Madame Alexander

Collector's Dolls
Price Guide

#18

Patricia R. Smith

COLLECTOR BOOKS

A Division of Schroeder Publishing Co., Inc.

The current values in this book should be used only as a guide. They are not intended to set prices, which vary from one section of the country to another. Auction prices as well as dealer prices vary greatly and are affected by condition as well as demand. Neither the Author nor the Publisher assumes responsibility for any losses that might be incurred as a result of consulting this guide.

Searching For A Publisher?

We are always looking for knowledgeable people considered to be experts within their fields. If you feel that there is a real need for a book on your collectible subject and have a large comprehensive collection, contact us.

COLLECTOR BOOKS
P.O. Box 3009
Paducah, Kentucky 42002-3009.

Printed by IMAGE GRAPHICS, INC., Paducah, Kentucky

Thank you ...

Linda Crowsey, Lahunta McIntyre, Chris McWilliams, and Helen Thomas for your help in making the prices in this volume more realistic, especially with the 8" dolls.

– *Patricia R. Smith*

PHOTO CREDITS

Lee Crane, Linda Crowsey, Frasher Doll Auctions, LeeAnn Geary, Green's Museum, Roger Jones, Kris Lundquist, Lahunta McIntyre, Ellen McCorkell, Chris McWilliams, "Flip" Phelps, Charmaine Shields, Martha Sweeny.

Cover: 8" Alexander-kins – "Cinderella" (1992) and "Snow White (1991).

ABOUT PRICING

Prices in this guide are based upon a *perfect* doll. An exceptional doll will bring higher prices and a doll that is less than perfect should be priced lower than price given.

The question most often asked is, "What is a perfect doll?" *Perfect* refers to doll and clothes only, with the following items present and necessary to warrant the statement, "This doll is perfect."

1. Outfit correct and complete on correct doll.
2. Doll and clothes must be in overall excellent, perfect condition.
3. Original hair set, hair shiny and perfect.
4. Overall eye appeal that allows for a scale in pricing.
5. All items present, such as hats, shoes, dog, toys, etc.
6. Tagged clothing in original condition, including Madame Alexander undergarments.
7. Unblemished coloring to doll and clothes. Facial coloring to your liking.
8. Properly functioning mechanisms, if walker, jointed, etc.
9. No broken lashes or pulled hair lashes.
10. No stains, shelf dust, rips, fading, moth holes, tears, cut tags, missing clothing, missing snaps, pulled elastic.
11. Clothes have not been laundered or ironed.
12. Eyes open and close properly.
13. No chipped lips, missing paint or scratches.
14. No glue marks around face, no cracks in doll's seams.

An *exceptional* doll would be better than a *perfect* doll. The following list shows what could add a greater price to an already perfect doll:

1. Wrist Tag.
2. Box.
3. Original price tag.
4. Rare clothing, color variation or hairstyle.
5. Autographed.
6. Madame Alexander boxed items that originally sold separately, such as coats, hats, glasses, etc., and given to original doll.
7. Unique, pristine, "tissue mint."
8. With wardrobe, trunk or case.

A *less than perfect* doll would be one with any of the following, and priced lower according to how many defects are present.

1. Not original tagged clothes in perfect condition.
2. Stains, spots, soil, shelf dust, any discoloration or fading.
3. Tears, rips, cuts, missing snaps, pulled or re-stitched elastic.
4. No tag or cut tag.
5. Re-dressed dolls.
6. Washed or dry cleaned clothes.

7. Hair mussed up, dirty, cut, pulled out places.
8. Glue marks around face or discolored face.
9. Missing items such as shoes, socks, hats, etc.
10. Replaced items.
11. Broken or cracked parts on body, fingers, limbs or head.
12. Missing eyelashes, broken eyelids.
13. Washed out face color, no cheek color, eyebrow paint missing or changed color.
14. Clothes not on correct year doll.
15. Mechanisms, such as walker, not functioning correctly.

If a scale were made to show a perfect, exceptional and less than perfect doll, it would look like this:

Less Than Perfect	PERFECT	Exceptional
Lowers Value		Adds Value

When buying Madame Alexander dolls, the main concern is *condition* of the doll and clothes. The Madame Alexander Doll Company designs fantastic clothes and the dolls are used to display clothes for a two-fold effect. One is artistic and the other is realistic, giving the full effect of doll and clothes for complete eye appeal. Therefore when purchasing a Madame Alexander doll, there must be perfect eye appeal to you, the buyer, along with a perfect doll and clothes.

There is no guarantee that *any* doll, antique or modern, will appreciate year after year. Prices remain high on exceptional dolls and always will. Much to the dismay of most of us, there always seems to be someone around who can and will spend the kind of money it takes to buy them. At times, the prices go higher on a plentiful perfect or exceptional doll due to the popularity of that particular doll.

What a person is willing to pay depends upon their financial resources and their willingness to spend. Because there are a great number of people who can and will spend large sums for a doll, it keeps the prices up, but not on all dolls, just on those particular ones. Since most people do have limited doll money, the rest of us want to be certain we are getting the most for our money.

There used to be new collectors who would buy less than perfect Madame Alexander dolls, but their ranks have slimmed down considerably. The majority of present day doll collectors want the best doll they can afford, with many willing to wait until they have the amount of funds available to buy one perfect Madame Alexander doll instead of several less than perfect ones. Collectors still buy for personal preference, individual eye appeal and think of investment in relation to the doll, with some buying for sentiment as it may have been the type of doll they had as a child or one their own children played with. No matter the reason, the most important factor is price versus condition. One more important reason for a purchase may be the collector's own need for their collection, such as to finish a certain set like the Sound of Music, Little Women, etc.

New collectors are being created each and every day by shoppers seeing and buying dolls from store shelves. Most of these people are totally unaware of "organized" doll collecting, such as clubs, publications, doll shows, etc. Starting in 1989, assistance has been provided for these beginners in the form of a card in each Alexander doll box, inviting them to join the Madame Alexander Doll Club (M.A.D.C.).

Collectors of "newer" Alexander dolls often branch out and begin buying older dolls through flea markets, shows and other secondary markets. These people should be aware of the following points:

1. Mold marks can be the same for an extended period of time. For example, 14" "Mary Ann" dolls will be marked "1965," which was the first year the doll was made. From then and until now, all "Mary Ann" face dolls will bear the 1965 mold number. Another example is the 21" "Jacqueline" doll, first introduced in 1961. Since 1965, all portraits have been based on the "Jacqueline" doll and bear the 1961 date. Determining the exact year any particular doll was made can be difficult for that reason.

2. Many times the Alexander Doll Company used the very same photographs to illustrate their catalogs, year after year. There are many variations of the same basic costume, especially in the 8" dolls and the only way an exact year for the particular doll can be found is in the booklet attached to the wrist of the doll. There can be, and are, many variations in costume during the year, depending on availability of colors and prints at the factory.

"Dealers" cannot pay price guide prices for dolls, as they must add expenses such as travel, booth rental, telephone calls, etc., and they must find a buyer, plus they must make a profit. The dealer has to consider all these things prior to making a purchase for resale. The dealer who is sensitive to the market realizes they must resell a doll based upon what they had to give for it, which depends upon the source they purchased from. Sometimes a dealer can resell below "book value," and at other times must get book values. Price guides are based on a doll being purchased from a dealer. A collector may search other sources to obtain dolls at lower prices, such as estate sales, ads in local papers, or by searching for dolls in out-of-the-way places. When discussing dealers, it must be noted that when dolls are purchased on a layaway plan versus cash, the layaway may be higher, but gives the collector the opportunity to own an exceptional doll.

Price guides must be based upon prices for a *perfect* doll and all collectors need accurate prices for insurance reasons. An insurance company or a postal service must have some means to appraise a damaged or stolen doll for the insuree, and the collector must have some means to judge their own collections to be able to purchase adequate amounts of insurance.

A price guide is a *guide* and not the "last word," as we ourselves have the "last word" in our own dealings. We do not have to pay an asking price unless we want the doll and can afford it.

Madame Alexander dolls will always be collectible and endure time and value. Beautiful dolls have flowed from this factory for over 65 years and will continue to do so. We hope all of you will continue to build the collections you so desire, be they older dolls or the excellent current dolls that become available each year.

Abbreviations are:
   hp – hard plastic
   Compo – composition
   C.U. – Collector United Newspaper
   F.A.D. – factory altered outfit
   SLNW – straight leg, non-walker
   SLW – straight leg walker
   BKW – bend knee walker
   BK – bend knee
   U.F.D.C. – United Federation of Doll Clubs
   M.A.D.C. - Madame Alexander Doll Club

The dolls named after real people are listed with last name first (Example: "Bliss, Betty Taylor"). Make-believe doll names will be listed with first name first (Example: "Tommy Snooks").

Some 8" International, Storybook Dolls, 21" Portraits, 10" Portrettes, babies, and 14" dolls are selling below suggested retail/catalog prices.

You can join the Madame Alexander Doll Club (M.A.D.C.) by writing 615 West 131st Street; New York, NY 10027.

THE MANY FACES OF MADAME ALEXANDER DOLLS

WENDY ANN (COMPO.)

TINY & LITTLE BETTY

PRINCESS ELIZABETH

MAGGIE

MARGARET (O'BRIEN)

CISSY

ELISE (1950's – 1960's)

LISSY

CISSETTE

MARY-BEL

JACQUELINE

MARY ANN

ELISE (1960's – 1980's)

POLLY & LESLIE

NANCY DREW

WENDY ANN – NEW 1988 FACE

MAGGIE MIXUP (1960–1961)

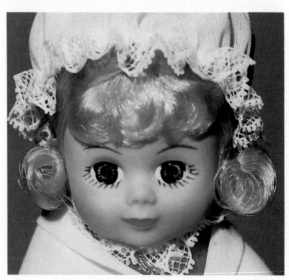

MAGGIE MIXUP (1988–1991)

Please read "About Pricing" for additional information.

ACTIVE MISS 18" hp., 1954 only, (Violet/Cissy) 675.00
ADAMS, ABIGAIL Presidents' Ladies/First Ladies Series, 1976–1978. First Set (Mary Ann) 120.00
ADAMS, LOUISA Presidents' Ladies/First Ladies Series, 1976–1978. First Set (Louisa) 120.00
AFRICA 8" hp., 1966–1971, BK (Wendy Ann)...300.00
    8" hp. straight leg re-issued 1988–1992, (Wendy Ann) 52.00
AGATHA 18" hp. (Cissy)
    Me and My Shadow Series. 1954 only, rose taffeta 1,350.00
    8" hp. (Wendy Ann) 1953–1954, black top and floral gown 1,500.00
    21" Portrait, #2171, 1967, red gown (Jacqueline) 525.00
        #2297, 1974, pink gown with full length cape (Jacqueline)..........................475.00
        #2291, 1975, blue with white sequin trim (Jacqueline) 400.00
        #2294, 1976, blue with white rick-rack trim (Jacqueline) 300.00
        #2230, 1979, 1980, 1981, lavender 285.00
        #2230, 1981, blue (Jacqueline) 275.00
    10" Portrette, #1171, 1968 only, red velvet (Cissette) 425.00
AGNES Cloth/felt, 1930's 650.00
ALASKA 8", Americana Series, 1990 (Maggie) 50.00
ALBANIA 8" straight leg, 1987 only (Wendy Ann) 80.00
ALEXANDER RAG TIME DOLLS Cloth, 1938–1939 only ....800.00 up
ALEXANDER-KINS 7½–8" hp., must have good face color (Wendy Ann)
If doll is not listed here, see regular listing for name. (Add more for mint or mint in box dolls. Special hairdos are higher priced.)
    Straight leg non-walker, 1953–1954. (First price is for 1953 strung doll.)

Coat/hat (dress)	400.00	325.00
Cotton dress/organdy pinafore	450.00	350.00
Cotton dress/cotton pinafore	450.00	350.00
Day in Country long gown	1,000.00	
Dresser/doll/wardrobe	1,900.00 up	
Easter doll	875.00	
Felt jackets/pleated skirt dresses	550.00	
Garden Party long gown	1,000.00 up	
Jumper/one pc. bodysuit	250.00	200.00
Nightgown	250.00	200.00
Nude/perfect doll (Excellent face color)	200.00	125.00
Organdy dress/cotton pinafore/hat	550.00	425.00
Organdy dress/organdy pinafore/hat	550.00	425.00
Satin dress/cotton pinafore/hat	550.00	425.00
Satin dress/organdy pinafore/hat	550.00	425.00
Sleeveless satin/organdy or cotton pinafore	450.00	350.00
Robe/nightgown or P.J.'s	300.00	225.00
Taffeta dress/cotton pinafore/hat	550.00	425.00

    Straight leg walker, 1955 only, must have good face color. (Add more for mint or mint in box dolls.)

Basic doll in box/panties/shoes/socks	275.00
Coat/hat (dress)	325.00
Cotton dress/pinafore	265.00
Cotton school dress	250.00
Garden Party long gown	985.00 up
Nude/perfect doll (Excellent face color)	175.00
Maypole Dance	345.00
Nightgown	150.00
Organdy party dress/hat	425.00

ALEXANDER-KIN, bend knee walker, 1956

ALEXANDER-KIN with wrist tag, 1960

P.J.'s 145.00
Riding Habit .... 375.00 up
Robe/nightgown or P.J.'s 145.00
Sailor dress 750.00
Sleeveless organdy dress 250.00
Swimsuits 225.00
Taffeta/satin party dress/hat 400.00
Bend knee walker, 1956–1964, must have good face color. (Add more for mint or mint in box dolls.)
Nude (Excellent face color) 125.00
Basic doll in box/panties/shoes/socks 225.00
Carcoat set 450.00
Cherry Twin (each) .... 1,200.00 up
Coat/hat 185.00
Cotton dress/cotton pinafore 250.00
Cotton or satin dress/organdy pinafore/hat 300.00
First Dancing dress (gown) 650.00
Felt jacket/pleated skirt/dress/cap or hat 325.00
Flowergirl .... 1,200.00 up
June Wedding 750.00
Long party dress .... 1,000.00 up
Taffeta party dress/hat 350.00
Nightgown/robe 175.00

Neiman-Marcus in case/all clothes (*Must be on correct doll/hairdo) 985.00
  *Name of store printed on material 650.00
  *2 pc. playsuit 375.00
  *Robe 175.00
Organdy dress/organdy pinafore/hat 325.00
Riding habit, corduroy, girl 400.00
  Riding habit, boy 425.00
  Devon Horse Show 600.00
Skater 475.00
Sleeveless school dress 225.00
Sundress 200.00
Swimsuits, beach outfits 200.00
Velvet party dress 850.00
Bend Knee, non-walkers, 1965–1972. (Add more for mint or mint in box dolls.)
  Basic doll in box with panties/shoes/socks 100.00
  Cotton dress, 1965 ....125.00
  Easter Egg/doll 1,500.00
  French Braid/cotton dress, 1965 ....200.00
  Felt jacket/skirt/dress/cap/hat, 1965 ....275.00
  Nude, perfect doll (Excellent face color) 50.00
  Organdy dress/hat, 1965 ....225.00
  Riding habit, check pants, girl, 1965 ....275.00
  Riding habit, check pants, boy, 1965 ....325.00
  Sewing kit/doll ....1,400.00 up
ALICE 18" hp., 1951 only (Maggie) 750.00
  8", Storyland Series, 1990 (Wendy Ann) 52.00
ALICE IN HER PARTY KIT 1965 only, (Mary Ann) 700.00
ALICE IN WONDERLAND
  16" cloth, 1930 and 1933 ....800.00
  7" compo., 1930's (Tiny Betty) 265.00
  9" compo., 1930's (Little Betty) 300.00
  11–14" compo., 1936–1940 (Wendy Ann) 465.00
  13" compo., swivel waist, 1930's (Wendy Ann) 450.00
  14½–18" compo., 1948–1949 (Margaret) 500.00
  21" compo., 1948–1949 (Margaret) 950.00
  15", 18", 21" compo., 1930's (Wendy Ann) 425.00–650.00
  14½" hp., 1949–1950 (Margaret) 625.00
  14" hp., 1950 (Maggie) 675.00
  17–23" hp. 1949–1950 (Maggie & Margaret) ....550.00–750.00 up
  15", 18", 23" hp., 1951–1952 (Maggie & Margaret) ....600.00, 700.00, 900.00 up
  14" hp. with trousseau, 1951–1952 (Maggie) ....1,300.00 up
  29" cloth/vinyl, 1952 (Barbara Jane) ....475.00 up
  29" vinyl, 1952 (Annabelle) ....575.00 up
  8" hp., 1955–1956 (Wendy Ann) 650.00
  12", 1963 (Lissy) 1,200.00
  14" plastic/vinyl, 1966–1992, Literature & Classic Series (Mary Ann) 74.00
  8" hp. Disney Crest Color, (Disneyland, Disney World), 1972–1976 ....500.00
  10", with white rabbit, 1991. (see Disney under Special Events/Exclusives)
ALCOTT, LOUISA MAY 14", Classic Series, 1989–1990 (Mary Ann) 80.00
  8" hp., Storyland Series, 1992 (Wendy Ann) 55.00
ALGERIA 8" straight leg, 1988 only, (Maggie) 90.00
ALLISON 18" cloth/vinyl, 1990–1991 only 100.00
ALPINE BOY AND GIRL Made for Christmas Shoppe, 1992 (see Special Events/Exclusives)
ALTAR BOY 8" hp., 1991 only, Americana Series 65.00

AMANDA 8" hp., 1961, Americana Series (Wendy Ann) 2,100.00
AMERICAN BABIES 16–18", cloth, 1930's 300.00
AMERICAN BEAUTY #1142, 10" Portrette, 1991–1992 ....80.00
AMERICAN GIRL 7–8" compo., 1938 (Tiny Betty) 265.00
    9–11" compo., 1937 (Little Betty, Wendy Ann) 300.00–400.00
    8" hp., 1962–1963, became "McGuffey Ana" in 1964-1965, (Wendy Ann) 385.00
AMERICAN INDIAN 9" compo., 1938–1939 (Little Betty) 300.00
AMERICAN TOTS 16–21", cloth dressed in child's fashions. 300.00–450.00
AMERICAN WOMEN'S VOLUNTEER SERVICE (AWVS) 14" compo., 1942 (Wendy Ann) 750.00
AMISH BOY 8" hp., BK, 1966–1969, Americana Series (Wendy Ann) 400.00
AMISH GIRL 8" hp. BK, 1966-1969, Americana Series (Wendy Ann) 400.00
AMY (see "Little Women").
ANASTASIA 10", 1988–1989, Portrette Series (Cissette) 75.00
ANATOLIA 8" straight leg, 1987–1988 ....50.00
ANGEL 8", in pink, blue, off-white gowns (Wendy & Maggie) 950.00
    8" Guardian, 1954 only, (Wendy Ann) 950.00
    8" Guardian, 1961 (Maggie Mixup) 985.00
    8" Baby, hp., 1955 (Wendy Ann) 985.00
ANGEL FACE 8" (see "Special Events/Exclusives")
ANNA BALLERINA 18" compo., Pavlova, 1940 (Wendy Ann) 1,100.00
ANNABELLE 14–15" hp., 1951–1952 only (Maggie) 500.00
    14–15" trousseau/trunk, 1952 only ....1,200.00 up
    18" hp., 1951–1952 ....575.00
    20–23" hp., 1951–1952 ....675.00
ANNABELLE AT CHRISTMAS (see Belks under Special Events/Exclusives)
ANNA KARENINA #2265, 21" Portrait, 1991 (Jacqueline) 335.00
ANNE OF GREEN GABLES 14", 1990 only (Mary Ann) 105.00
    14", reintroduced 1992, with trunk/wardrobe (Louisa/Jennifer) 225.00
    14", Arrives At Station, 1992 ....142.00
        White organdy dress only, 1992 ....50.00
        Puff sleeve dress only, 1992 ....45.00
        Winter coat outfit only, 1992 ....50.00
ANNIE LAURIE 14" compo., 1937 (Wendy Ann) 675.00
    17" compo., 1937 (Wendy Ann) 985.00
ANTOINETTE 21" compo., 1946 (Wendy Ann) 2,100.00
ANTONY, MARK 12", 1980–1985, Portraits of History (Nancy Drew) 65.00
APPLE ANNIE 8" hp., 1954 (Wendy Ann) 1,250.00
APPLE PIE 14", Classics, 1991 only (Mary Ann) 85.00
APRIL 14", Doll Classics, 1990–1991 (Mary Ann & Jennifer) 95.00
ARGENTINE BOY 8" hp., BKW & BK, 1965 only (Wendy Ann) 375.00
ARGENTINE GIRL 8" hp., BK, 1965–1972 (Wendy Ann) 125.00
    BKW (Wendy Ann) 175.00
    8" hp., straight legs, 1973–1976, marked "Alex" 60.00
    8" hp., straight legs, 1976–1986 (1985–1986 white face) 55.00
ARMENIA 8" 1989–1990 (Wendy Ann) 50.00
ARRIVING IN AMERICA 8" hp., 1992, Americana Series (Wendy Ann) 55.00
ARTIE 12" plastic/vinyl, 1962, sold through FAO Schwarz (Smarty) 275.00
ASHLEY 8", 1990, Scarlett Series, tan jacket/hat 70.00
    8" hp., Conferate Officer, Scarlett Series, 1991 ....55.00
ASTOR 9", early vinyl toddler, 1953 only, gold organdy dress & bonnet 95.00
ASTROLOGICAL MONTH DOLLS 14–17" compo., 1938 (Wendy) 500.00
AUNT AGATHA 8" hp., 1957 (Wendy Ann) 1,200.00
AUNT BETSY Cloth/felt, 1930's 850.00

AUNT PITTY PAT   14–17" compo., 1939 (Wendy Ann) 1,900.00
   8" hp., 1957 (Wendy Ann)...1,800.00
   8" hp., straight leg, 1991–1992, Scarlett Series 57.00
AUSTRALIA   8", 1990–1991 only (Wendy Ann) 55.00
AUSTRIA BOY*   8" hp., 1974–1992 (Wendy Ann)
   Straight legs, 1973–1975, marked "Alex"...60.00
   1976-1989, marked "Alexander" (1985–1987 white face) 55.00
AUSTRIA GIRL*   8" hp., 1974–1992 (Wendy Ann)
   Straight legs, 1973–1975, marked "Alex." 60.00
   1976–1990, marked "Alexander" (1985–1987 white face) 55.00
AUTUMN IN N.Y.   (see first Modern Doll Club under "Special Events/Exclusives")
AVRIL, JANE   10" (see "Special Events/Exclusives")

* *Formerly* TYROLEAN BOY AND GIRL

AUSTRIA **from 1984 on left; 1986 on right**

Please read "About Pricing" for additional information.

Babbie   Cloth with long thin legs, inspired by Katherine Hepburn. 850.00
    16", cloth child doll, 1934–1936 ....600.00
    14" hp. (Maggie) 600.00
Babs   20" hp., 1949 (Maggie) 625.00
Babs Skater   15" hp., 1948–1950 (Margaret) 575.00
    17–18" hp. 585.00
    21" hp. 600.00
    18" compo. (Margaret) 750.00
Babette   10", Portrette Series, 1988–1989 (Cissette) 75.00
Babsie Baby   Compo./cloth, moving tongue 400.00
Babsie Skater (roller)   15", 1941 (Princess Elizabeth) 700.00
Baby Betty   10–12" compo., 1935–1936 ....250.00
Baby Brother and Sister   20", cloth/vinyl, 1977–1979 (Mary Mine) ....75.00 each
    14", 1979–1982 ....80.00 each
    14", re-introduced   1989 only ....60.00 each
Baby Clown   8" hp., painted face, 1955 (Wendy Ann) 1,700.00
Baby Ellen   14", 1965–1972 (Black Sweet Tears) 100.00
Baby Genius   11", all cloth, 1930's 450.00
    11–12" compo./cloth, 1930's–1940's 165.00
    16" compo./cloth, 1930's–1940's 175.00
    15", 18", 21" hp. head, vinyl limbs, 1949–1950 ....80.00–100.00
    8" hp./vinyl, 1956–1962 (see Little Genius)
Baby Jane   16" compo., 1935 ....875.00 up
Baby Lynn   20" cloth/vinyl, 1973–1976 ....100.00
Baby McGuffey   22–24" compo., 1937 ....165.00
    20" cloth/vinyl, 1971–1976 ....175.00
    14" cloth/vinyl, 1972–1978 ....165.00

14" Baby McGuffey, 1940's

BABY PRECIOUS 14" cloth/vinyl, 1975 only 70.00
    21" cloth/vinyl, 1974–discontinued 1976 ....90.00
BABY IN LOUIS VUITTON TRUNK/WARDROBE Any year ....750.00 up
BAD LITTLE GIRL 16" cloth, 1966 only, blue dress (Mate to "Good Little Girl") 90.00
BALLERINA (Also see individual dolls – Leslie, Margaret, etc.)
    9" compo., 1935–1941 (Little Betty) 300.00
    11–13", 1930's (Betty) 250.00–350.00
    11–14" compo., 1936–1938 (Wendy Ann) 265.00–275.00
    17" compo., 1938–1941 (Wendy Ann) 500.00
    21" compo., "Deborah" ("Debra"), Portrait ballerina, 1947 (Wendy Ann) 2,300.00
    8" hp. (Wendy Ann)
        SLNW, Lavender, Yellow, Pink, 1953–1954 ....550.00
            Blue 550.00
        SLW, Lavender, Yellow, Pink, 1955 ....565.00
            Blue 500.00
    BKW, Golden Yellow, 1954–1960 ....525.00
        Blue, 1957 ....400.00
        Rose, 1956 ....550.00
        Lavender, 1961 ....600.00
        Gold, 1959 ....575.00
        Pink, 1958 ....225.00
        Yellow, 1956 ....500.00
        White, 1955 ....400.00

8" BALLERINA, 1955

BK, Yellow, 1965–1972 ....375.00
    Blue, 1962–1972 ....225.00
    Pink, 1962–1972 ....200.00
8" straight leg, 1973–1992 (1985–1987 white face) 60.00
8" Enchanted Doll House (see Special Events/Exclusive)
8", Americana Series, white/gold, 1990–1991 (Wendy Ann) (Black or white dolls, 1991)..............65.00
    1992, pink, black or white doll (Wendy Ann) 52.00
8", M.A.D.C., 1984 (see Special Events/Exclusives)
10–11" hp. (Cissette) 1957–1959 ....425.00
12", 1964 only (Janie) 300.00
12", "Muffin," 1989–1990 (Janie) 70.00
12", Romance Collection, 1990–1992 (Nancy Drew) 72.00
14" hp., "Binnie," 1956 (15" & 18", 1956 only) (Cissy)...285.00
14" plastic/vinyl, 1973–1982 (Mary Ann) 165.00
14", 1963 only (Melinda) ....375.00 up
15–18" hp., 1950–1952 (Margaret) 385.00–475.00
16½" hp., 1957, 1958, 1959, 1962 (Elise) 350.00
    1963 only (Marybel) (18" also Elise) 350.00
17" plastic/vinyl, discontinued costume, 1967–1989 (Elise)...95.00
17" plastic/vinyl, "Firebird" and "Swan Lake," 1990–1991 (Elise)..125.00
17", 1970–1971 only (Leslie)...325.00

1987 Portrait SARAH BERNHARDT

Rare 12" BETTY of 1936

BARBARA JANE 29" cloth/vinyl, 1952 only 400.00
BARBARY COAST 10" hp., Portrette Series, 1962–1963 (Cissette) ....1,200.00 up
BARTON, CLARA 10", Portrette Series, 1989 only (Cissette)...75.00
BEAU ART DOLLS 18" hp., 1953 only (Margaret, Maggie) ....1,400.00 up
BEAU BRUMMEL Cloth, 1930's 725.00
BEAUTY 12", 1992, Romance Series (Nancy Drew) 105.00
BEAST 12", 1992, Romance Series (Nancy Drew) 115.00
BEAUTY QUEEN 10" hp., 1961 only (Cissette) 225.00
BEDDY BYE BROOKE FAO Schwarz (see Special Events/Exclusives)
BELLE BRUMMEL Cloth, 1930's 725.00
BELLE OF THE BALL 10", Portrette Series, 1989 only (Cissette) 75.00
BELLOWS' ANNE 14" plastic/vinyl, Fine Arts Series, 1987 only 75.00
BELGIUM 8" hp., BK, 1972 only (Wendy Ann) 100.00
    8" straight legs, 1973–1975, marked "Alex" 60.00
    8" straight legs, 1976–1988, marked "Alexander" (1985–1987 white face) 55.00
    7" compo., 1935–1938 (Tiny Betty) 245.00
BELK DEPARTMENT STORES (see Special Events/Exclusives)
BELLE WATLING 10", 1992, Scarlett Series (Cissette) 90.00
BERNHARDT, SARAH #2249, 21", dressed in all burgundy, 1987 only 250.00
BESSY BELL 14" plastic/vinyl, Classic Series, 1988 only (Mary Ann) 70.00
BESSY BROOKS 8", Storybook Series, 1988–1991 (Wendy Ann) 55.00
    8", 1990, C.U. Gathering (see Special Events/Exclusives)
BEST MAN 8" hp., 1955 only (Wendy Ann) 750.00
BETH (see "Little Women")
    10", Spiegel's (Cissette) (see Special Events/Exclusives)
BETTY 14" compo., 1935–1942 ....325.00
    12" compo., 1936–1937 only 400.00
    16–18" compo., 1935–1942 ....375.00–425.00
    19–21" compo., 1938–1941 ....375.00–500.00
    14½–17½" hp., made for Sears in 1951 only (Maggie) 485.00–585.00
    30" plastic/vinyl, 1960 only 385.00
BETTY, TINY 7" compo., 1934–1943 ....250.00
BETTY, LITTLE 9" compo, 1935–1943 ....295.00
BETTY BAG All cloth, flat painted face, yarn hair, 1940's 300.00
BETTY BLUE 8" straight leg, 1987–1988 only, Storybook Series (Maggie) 60.00
BIBLE CHARACTER DOLLS 8" hp., 1954 (Wendy Ann) ....each 5,200.00 up
BILL/BILLY 8" hp., boys clothes and hair style, 1955–1963 (Wendy Ann) 375.00
    Groom, 1953–1957 ....525.00
BINNIE WALKER 15–18" hp., 1954–1955 only (Cissy) 95.00–185.00
    15" in trunks/wardrobe, 1955 only 400.00
    15" Skater, hp., 1955 only 285.00
    18" Toddler, plastic/vinyl, 1964 only 325.00
    25" Informals, 1955 only 475.00
    25" hp., 1954–1955 only 385.00
BIRTHDAY DOLLS 7" compo. (Tiny Betty)..250.00
BIRTHDAY, HAPPY M.A.D.C., 1985 (see Special Events/Exclusives)
BITSEY 11–12" compo., 1942–1946 ....125.00
    11–16", head hp., 1949–1951 ....70.00–95.00
    19–26", 1949–1951..125.00–145.00
    12" cloth/vinyl, 1965–1966 only 75.00
BITSEY, LITTLE 9" all vinyl, 1967–1968 only 95.00
    11–16" 30.00–175.00
BLACK FOREST 8", 1989–1991 (Wendy Ann) 60.00–105.00

BLISS, BETTY TAYLOR 2nd set First Ladies/Presidents' Ladies Series, 1979–1981 (Mary Ann)............105.00
BLUE BOY 16" cloth, 1930's 800.00
    7" compo., 1936–1938 (Tiny Betty) 285.00
    9" compo., 1938–1941 (Little Betty) 300.00
    12" plastic/vinyl, Portrait Children, 1972–1983 (Nancy Drew) 70.00
        In blue velvet, 1985–1987 ....70.00
BLUE DANUBE 18" hp., 1953 only, pink floral gown (Margaret)......................................1,200.00 up
    18" hp., blue taffeta, Me and My Shadow Series, 1954 only (Margaret)............1,200.00 up
BLUE MOON 14", Classic Series, 1991–1992 (Louisa) 170.00
BLUE ZIRCON 10", 1992, Birthday Collection..64.00
BOBBY 8" hp., 1957 only (Wendy Ann) 465.00
    8" hp., 1960 only (Maggie Mixup)...500.00
BOBBY Q. Cloth, 1940–1942 ....625.00
BOBBY SOXER 8" hp., for Disney, 1990–1991 (see Special Events/Exclusives)
BOBO CLOWN 8", 1991–1992, (Wendy Ann) 52.00
BOHEMIA 8", 1989–1991 (Wendy Ann) 55.00
BOLIVIA 8" hp., BK & BKW, 1963–1966 (Wendy Ann) 550.00
BONNIE (BABY) 16–19" vinyl, 1954–1955 ....80.00
    24–30", 1954–1955 ....135.00–165.00
BONNIE BLUE #1305, 14", Jubilee II, 1989 only (Mary Ann) 95.00
    8" hp., 1990–1992 (Wendy Ann) 57.00
BONNIE TODDLER 18" cloth/hp. head/vinyl limbs, 1950–1951 ....110.00
    19" all vinyl, 1954–1955 ....145.00
BOONE, DANIEL 8" hp., Americana Series, has no knife (Wendy Ann) 60.00
BO PEEP, LITTLE 7" compo., Storybook Series, 1937–1941 (Tiny Betty)........................275.00
    9–11" compo., 1936–1940 (Little Betty, Wendy Ann) 285.00–325.00
    7½" hp., SLW, 1955 (Wendy Ann) 485.00
    8" hp., BKW, 1962–1964 (Wendy Ann) 375.00
    8" hp., BK, 1965–1972 (Wendy Ann) 135.00
    8" hp., straight leg, 1973–1975, marked "Alex" (Wendy Ann).................................60.00
    8" hp., 1976–1986, marked "Alexander" (1985–1986 white face) (Wendy Ann) 55.00
    14", 1988–1989, Classic Series (Mary Ann) 60.00
    14", reintroduced 1992, candy stripe pink (Mary Ann) 132.00
    12" porcelain, #009, 1990–1992 ....255.00
BRAZIL 7" compo., 1937–1943 (Tiny Betty) 225.00
    9" compo. (Little Betty) 1938–1940 ....250.00
    8" hp., BKW, 1965–1972 (Wendy Ann) 250.00
      BK 100.00
    8" hp., straight leg, 1973–1975, marked "Alex." (Wendy Ann)................................60.00
    8" hp., straight leg, 1976–1988, marked "Alexander" (1985–1987 white face) 55.00
      1985–1987 white face 50.00
BRENDA STARR 12" hp., 1964 only (became "Yolanda" in 1965) 200.00
    Bride..200.00
    Street dresses 175.00
    Ball gown 225.00
    Beach outfit 185.00
    Raincoat/hat/dress 225.00
BRIAR ROSE 8", M.A.D.C. (see Special Events/Exclusives)
BRIDE 7" compo., 1935–1939 (Tiny Betty)..250.00
    9–11" compo., 1936–1941 (Little Betty) 265.00–325.00
    13", 14", 15" compo., 1935–1941 (Wendy Ann)....................................250.00–275.00
    17–18" compo., 1935–1943 (Wendy Ann) 400.00
    21–22" compo., 1942–1943 (Wendy Ann) 585.00
      In trunk/trousseau, compo. (Wendy Ann).......................................1,400.00 up

21" compo., Royal Wedding/Portrait, 1945–1947 ....2,000.00 up
15" hp., 1951–1955 (Margaret) 575.00
17" hp., 1950, in pink (Margaret) 650.00
18" hp., tagged "Prin. Elizabeth" (Margaret) 600.00
18" hp., 1949–1955 (Maggie, Margaret) 575.00
21" hp., 1949–1953 (Margaret, Maggie) 675.00
23" hp. 1949, 1952–1955 (Margaret) 675.00
25" hp., 1955 only (Margaret)...700.00
16½" hp. 1957–1964, 18" in 1963 only (Elise)..300.00
20" hp., 1955–1958 (Cissy)
   1955 only, brocade gown with floor length veil, Dreams Come True Series 475.00
   1956 only, tulle gown, tulle cap & chapel length veil 475.00
   1957 only, nylon tulle with double train of satin, Models Formal Gowns Series 500.00
   1958 only, lace circles near hem, Dolls To Remember Series 575.00
10" hp., 1957–1963 (Cissette) 245.00
10" hp., in trunk/trousseau, various years (Cissette) ....900.00 up
10", Portrette Series, 1990–1991 (Cissette) 100.00
12" hp., 1956–1959 (Lissy) 250.00

**21" rare BRIDE using the Wendy Ann doll.
All composition, mint and original.**

**17" BRIDESMAID using the Elise doll.
1987**

12" porcelain, 1991–1992 (version of 14" head) 255.00
21", #2151, Portrait, full lace, wide lace edge on veil, 1965 (Jacqueline) 900.00
   #2192, full lace overskirt, plain veil, 1969 ....775.00
8" hp., 1953 only, Quizkin (Wendy Ann) 550.00
   1955–1958 ....325.00
   1960 ....300.00
   1963–1965, BKW 250.00
   1966–1972, BK 150.00
   1973–1975, straight leg, marked "Alex." 60.00
   1976–1992, straight leg, marked "Alexander" (1985–1987 white face) 55.00
   1985–1987 white face 45.00
8", factory altered for C.U. (see Special Events/Exclusives)
14" plastic/vinyl, 1973–1976 (Mary Ann) 75.00
14" plastic/vinyl, 1987–1990, Classic Series (Mary Ann, Jennifer) 95.00
14", reintroduced 1992, ecru gown (Louisa) 165.00
17" plastic/vinyl, 1966–1988 (Elise) 125.00
17" plastic/vinyl, 1966–1971 (Leslie) 250.00
17" plastic/vinyl, 1965–1970 (Polly) 300.00
21" porcelain, 1989–1990 ....510.00
BRIDESMAID 9" compo., 1937–1939 (Little Betty) 265.00
   11–14" compo., 1938–1942 (Wendy Ann)..250.00–425.00
   15–18" compo., 1939–1944 (Wendy Ann)..350.00–450.00
   20–22" compo., Portrait, 1941–1947 (Wendy Ann)...2,000.00
   21½" compo., 1938–1941 (Prin. Elizabeth) 1,000.00
   15–17" hp., 1950–1952 (Margaret, Maggie) 425.00–575.00
   15" hp., 1952 (Maggie)..425.00
   18" hp., 1952 (Maggie)..600.00

BRIDE, GROOM, and BRIDESMAID, all from 1957.

19" rigid vinyl, in pink, 1952–1953 (Margaret) 550.00
15" hp., 1955 only (Cissy, Binnie)..275.00
18" hp., 1955 only (Cissy, Binnie)..375.00
25" hp., 1955 only (Cissy, Binnie)..500.00
20" hp., 1956 only, blue nylon tulle & net, Fashion Parade Series (Cissy) 500.00
10" hp., 1957–1963 (Cissette)..450.00
12" hp., 1956–1959 (Lissy)..425.00
16½" hp., 1957–1959 (Elise)..425.00
8" hp., SLW, 1955 (Wendy Ann) 550.00
   1956, BKW 650.00
   1957–1958 BKW 650.00
17" (see Formals: Elise)
17" plastic/vinyl, 1966–1971 (Leslie)...250.00
BRIGITTA 11" & 14" (see "Sound of Music"). (Cissette, Mary Ann)
BROOKE 14", made for FAO Schwarz, 1989 (see Special Event/Exclusive)
BUCK RABBIT Cloth/felt, 1930's 600.00
BUD 16–19" cloth/vinyl, 1952 only (Rosebud head)..80.00
19" & 25", 1952–1953 only 130.00
BULGARIA 8", 1986–1987 (Wendy Ann) (white face) 55.00
BUMBLE BEE 8" hp., Americana Series, 1992 ....50.00
BUNNY 18" plastic/vinyl, 1962 only..250.00
BURMA 7" compo., 1939–1943 (Tiny Betty) 250.00
BUTCH 11–12" compo./cloth, 1942–1946...150.00
14–16" compo./cloth, 1949–1951 ....125.00–150.00
14" cloth, vinyl head & limbs, 1950 only 100.00–125.00
12" cloth/vinyl, 1965–1966 only 75.00
BUTCH, LITTLE 9" all vinyl, 1967–1968 only 125.00
BUTCH MCGUFFEY 22" compo./cloth, 1940–1941 ....200.00

Please read "About Pricing" for additional information.

C.U. (see Collector's United under Special Events/Exclusives)

CAMEO LADY 10" C.U., 1991 (see Special Events/Exclusives)

CAMELOT C.U. (see Special Events/Exclusives)

CAMILLE 21" compo., 1938–1939 (Wendy Ann) 2,000.00

CANADA 8" hp., BK, 1968–1972 (Wendy Ann)..115.00
    1973–1975, straight leg, marked "Alex."..60.00
    1976–1988, straight legs, marked "Alexander" (1985–1987 white face) 55.00
    1986, white face 55.00

CAPTAIN HOOK 8" hp., 1992 (Wendy Ann)..65.00

CARMEN (Dressed like Carmen Miranda, but not marked or meant as such.)
    7" compo., 1938–1943 (Tiny Betty) 275.00
    9–11" compo., boy & girl, 1938–1943 (see also "Rumbero/Rumbera") (Little Betty) ...each 265.00–300.00
    11" compo., sleep eyes, 1937–1939 (Little Betty) 285.00
    11–13" compo., 1937–1940 (Wendy Ann) 350.00
    15–18" compo., 1939–1942 (Wendy Ann) 465.00
    21" compo., 1939–1942 (Wendy Ann) 1,700.00
    14" plastic/vinyl, 1983–1986, Opera Series (Mary Ann) 90.00

CARNVALE DOLL FAO Schwarz, 1991 (see Special Events/Exclusives)

CARNIVAL IN RIO 21" porcelain, 1989–1990 ....460.00

CARNIVAL IN VENICE 21" porcelain, 1990–1991 ....525.00

CAROLINE 15" vinyl, 1961–1962 only, in dresses, pants/jacket 285.00
    In riding habit 350.00
    As boy/boy hairstyle (nude) 75.00
    In case/wardrobe ....1,400.00 up

14" CARMEN, 1983–1986   **14" CAREEN, 1992 Scarlett Series**

CARREEN 14–17" compo., 1937–1938 (Wendy Ann) 700.00
    14" plastic/vinyl, 1992 (Louisa/Jennifer) 132.00
CARROT TOP 21" cloth, 1967 only 85.00
CASSOCK 8" hp., 1989–1991 (Wendy Ann) 60.00
CATHY 17–21" compo., 1939, 1946 (Wendy Ann) 750.00
CELIA'S DOLLS (see Special Events/Exclusives)
CENTURY OF FASHIONS 14" & 18" hp., 1954 (Margaret, Maggie & Cissy) 1,300.00–1,500.00
CHARITY 8" hp., 1961 only, Americana Series (Wendy Ann) 2,100.00
CHARLENE 18" cloth/vinyl, 1991–1992 ....105.00
CHATTERBOX 24" plastic/vinyl, talker, 1961 only 200.00
CHEERLEADER 8", Americana Series, 1990–1991 only, (Wendy Ann) 55.00
    8", 1990 (see I. Magnin in Special Events/Exclusives)
    8" hp., black or white doll, Americana Series, 1992, royal blue/gold outfit 52.00
CHERI 18" hp., 1954 only, white satin gown, pink opera coat, Me & My Shadow Series (Margaret) 1,300.00
CHERRY TWINS 8" hp., 1957 only (Wendy Ann) each ....each 1,200.00 up
CHERUB 12" vinyl, 1960–1961 ....85.00
    18" hp. head/cloth & vinyl 90.00
    26" 125.00
CHERUB BABIES Cloth, 1930's 475.00
CHILE 8" hp., 1992 (Wendy Ann) 55.00
CHILD AT HEART SHOP 8" Easter Bunny, 1990 (see Special Events/Exclusives)
CHINA 7" compo., 1936–1940 (Tiny Betty) 250.00
    9" compo., 1935–1938 (Little Betty) 265.00

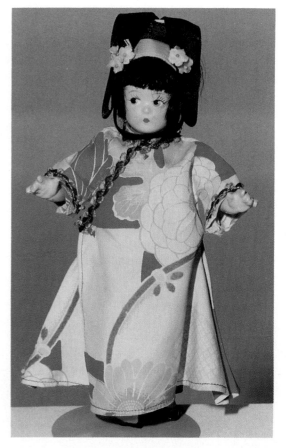

CENTURY OF FASHION using the Margaret doll   **7" CHINA using Tiny Betty. (Prints can vary)**

8" hp., BK, 1972 (Wendy Ann) 125.00
8" (Maggie Mixup) 150.00
Straight leg, 1973–1975, marked "Alex." 60.00
Straight legs, 1976–1986, marked "Alexander" 55.00
    1987–1989 (Maggie) 55.00
CHRISTENING BABY 11–13" cloth/vinyl, 1951–1954 ....75.00
    16–19" 100.00
CHRISTMAS SHOPPE (see Special Events/Exclusive)
CHRISTMAS CAROLING 10", Portrette Series, 1992 ....105.00
CHRISTMAS COOKIE 14", 1992 (Louisa/Jennifer) 115.00
CHRISTMAS TREE TOPPER 1991 Spiegel's (see Special Events/Exclusive)
CHURCHILL, LADY 18" hp., 1953, only Beaux Arts Series (Margaret) ....1,200.00 up
CHURCHILL, SIR WINSTON 18" hp., 1953 only (Margaret) 1,100.00
CINDERELLA 7–8" compo., 1935–1944 (Tiny Betty) 250.00
    9" compo., 1936–1941 (Little Betty) 285.00
    13" compo., 1935–1937 (Wendy Ann) 365.00
    14" compo., Sear's exclusive, 1939 only (Princess Elizabeth) 400.00
    15" compo., 1935–1937 (Betty) 450.00
    16–18" compo., 1935–1939 (Princess Elizabeth) 475.00–575.00
    8" hp., 1955 only (Wendy Ann) 750.00
    8" hp., Storyland Series, 1990–1991 (Wendy Ann) 55.00

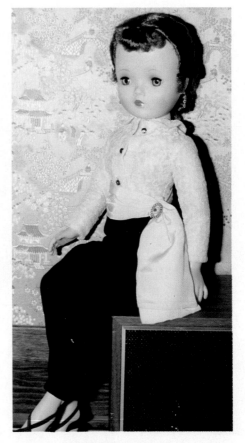

8" CINDERELLA, 1992   **20" CISSY, 1957**

8", 1992, blue ballgown 65.00
8", 1992, "poor" outfit in blue w/black strips 55.00
12" hp., 1966 only, Literature Series (classic Lissy) 1,200.00
14" hp., 1950–1951, ballgown (Margaret) 700.00
14" hp., 1950–1951, "Poor" outfit (Margaret) 650.00
18" hp., 1950–1951 (Margaret) 675.00
14" plastic/vinyl, 1967–1992, "poor" outfit (can be green, blue, gray or brown) (Mary Ann) 92.00
14" plastic/vinyl, 1970–1983, dressed in pink, Classic Series (Mary Ann) 75.00
    1984–1986, blue ballgown, two styles (Mary Ann) 85.00
14" 1987–1991, Classic Series, white ballgown (Mary Ann, Jennifer) 132.00
14" 1992, white/gold ballgown (Jennifer) 132.00
10", 1989, Disney World (see Special Events/Exclusives)
10", 1990–1991, Portrette Series, all pink (Cissette) 75.00
CISSETTE   10–11" hp. in various street dresses, 1957–1963 .... 200.00
  In formals 450.00
  Coats & hat 285.00
  Beauty queen with trophy, 1961 only 225.00
  Special gift set/three wigs .... 1,200.00 up
     Doll only. Clean, good face color 100.00
  Queen/trunk/trousseau, 1954 .... 850.00

10" CISSETTE in ballgown

CISSY   20" hp. (also 21"), 1955–1959, good face color, in various street dresses 250.00
  In ballgowns 775.00
  Trunk/wardrobe .... 1,400.00 up
  Magazine ads using doll, 1950's 7.00
CIVIL WAR   18" hp., 1953 only, Glamour Girls Series (Margaret) 1,300.00
  8" hp., 1953–1954 (Wendy Ann) 1,100.00
CLARA & THE NUTCRACKER   14" (Louisa/Jennifer) 90.00

CLARABELLE CLOWN 19", 1951–1953 ....385.00
   29" 600.00
   49" 750.00
CLAUDETTE 10", Portrette Series, 1988–1989 (Cissette) 70.00
CLEOPATRA 12", Portraits of History Series, 1980–1985 ....60.00
CLEVELAND, FRANCES 1985–1987, 4th set First Ladies/Presidents' Ladies Series (Mary Ann) 90.00
CLOVER KID 7" compo., 1935–1936 (Tiny Betty) 275.00
CLOWN 8", Americana Series, painted face, 1990–1991 (Maggie) 52.00
   BOBO, 8" hp., 1991–1992 (Wendy Ann) 52.00
   STILTS, 8" doll on stilts, 1992 ....60.00
COCO 21" plastic/vinyl, 1966, in various clothes other than Portrait 2,300.00
   10", Portrette Series, 1989–1992 (Cissette) 74.00
COLLECTOR UNITED DOLLS (see Special Events/Exclusives)
COLLEEN 10", Portrette Series, 1988 only (Cissette) 75.00
COLONIAL 7" compo., 1937–1938 (Tiny Betty) 265.00
   9" compo., 1936–1939 (Little Betty) 285.00
   8" hp., BKW, 1962–1964 (Wendy Ann) 365.00
CONFEDERATE OFFICER 12", Scarlett Series, 1990–1991 (Wendy Ann) 80.00
   8" hp., 1992–1992, Scarlett Series (see Ashley)
COOKIE 19" compo./cloth, 1938–1940 ....500.00
COOLIDGE, GRACE 14", 6th set Presidents' Ladies/First Ladies Series, 1989–1990 (Louisa) 100.00
CORNELIA #2191, 21", Portrait Series, 1972, dressed in pink with full cape (Jacqueline) 575.00
   #2191, 1973, pink with ¾–length jacket 500.00
   #2296, 1974, blue with black trim 400.00
   #2290, 1975, rose red with black trim and hat..400.00
   #2293, 1976, pink with black trim and hat 350.00

COCO, 1966 only

#2212, 1978, blue with full cape 325.00
Cloth/felt, 1930's 700.00
COUNTRY CHRISTMAS 14", Classic Series, 1991–1992 (Mary Ann) 132.00
COUNTRY COUSINS 10" cloth, 1940's 275.00
    26" cloth, 1940's 475.00
    30" cloth, 1940's 675.00
    16½", 1958 (Marybel) 225.00
COURTNEY AND FRIENDS (see Alexander Doll Co. under Special Events/Exclusives)
COUSIN GRACE 8" hp., BKW, 1957 only (Wendy Ann).....................................1,900.00
COUSIN KAREN 8" hp., BKW, 1956 only (Wendy Ann).....................................1,800.00
COUSIN MARIE & MARY 8" hp., 1963 only (Wendy Ann)..................each 1,200.00
COWBOY 8" hp., BK, Americana Series, 1967–1969 (Wendy Ann) 350.00
    8", 1987 (see M.A.D.C. under Special Events/Exclusives)
COWGIRL 8" hp., BK, Americana/Storybook Series, 1967–1979 (Wendy Ann)......350.00
    10", Portrette Series, 1990–1991 (Cissette) 75.00
CRETE 8" straight leg, 1987 only (white face) 55.00
CROCKETT, DAVY BOY OR GIRL 8" hp., 1955 only (Wendy Ann) 650.00
CRY DOLLY 14–16" vinyl. 12 pc. layette, 1953 ....125.00–175.00
    14", 16", 19" in swimsuit 65.00–125.00
    16–19" all vinyl, dress or rompers 80.00–145.00
CUDDLY 10½" cloth, 1942–1944 ....325.00
    17" cloth, 1942–1944 ....375.00
CURLY LOCKS 8" hp., 1955 only (Wendy Ann) 850.00
    8" straight leg, 1987–1988, Storybook Series 70.00
CYNTHIA 15" hp., 1952 only (Black Margaret) 950.00
    18", 1952 only 1,000.00
    23", 1952 only 1,300.00
CZECHOSLOVAKIA 8" hp., BK, 1972, (Wendy Ann) 135.00
    1973–1975, straight leg, marked "Alex." 60.00
    1976–1987, straight leg, marked "Alexander" 55.00
    8" white face, 1985–1987 ....55.00
    8", reintroduced 1992 (Wendy Ann)..55.00
    7" compo., 1935–1937 (Tiny Betty) 235.00

CURLY LOCKS, 1955

Please read "About Pricing" for additional information.

DAFFY DOWN DILLEY 8" straight legs, 1986 only, Storybook Series (Wendy Ann) 90.00
    8", Storybook Series, 1987–1989 (Maggie) 75.00
DAHL, ARLENE 18" hp., 1950–1951 (Maggie) ....3,400.00 up
DAISY 10", 1987–1989, Portrette Series (Cissette) 75.00
DANISH 7" compo., 1937–1941 (Tiny Betty) 265.00
    9" compo., 1938–1940 (Little Betty) 285.00
DARE, VIRGINIA 9" compo., 1940–1941 (Little Betty) 300.00
DARLENE 18" cloth/vinyl, 1991–1992 ....105.00
DAVID & DIANE 8", FAO Schwarz, 1989 (see Special Events/Exclusives)
DAVID COPPERFIELD 7" compo., 1936–1938 (Tiny Betty) 325.00
    14" compo., 1938 only (Wendy Ann) 750.00
    16" cloth Dicken's character, early 1930's 700.00–800.00
DAVID, LITTLE RABBI Celia's Dolls, 1991 (see Special Events/Exclusives)
DAVID QUACK-A-FIELD OR TWISTAIL Cloth/felt, 1930's 675.00
DAY OF WEEK DOLLS 7", 1935–1940 (Tiny Betty) ....each 265.00
    9–11" compo., 1936–1938 (Little Betty) ....each 300.00
    13" compo., 1939 (Wendy Ann) 450.00
DECEMBER 14", 1989 only, Classic Series (Mary Ann) 95.00
DEAREST 12" vinyl baby, 1962–1964 ....100.00
DEBUTANTE 18" hp., 1953 only (Maggie) 950.00
DEFOE, DR. 14" compo., 1937–1939 ....1,400.00
    15–16" compo., 1937–1939 ....1,500.00
DEGAS 21" compo., 1945–1946, Portrait (Wendy Ann) ....2,000.00 up
DEGAS GIRL 14" plastic/vinyl, 1967–1987, Portrait Children & Fine Art Series (Mary Ann) 75.00
DENMARK 10" hp., 1962–1963 (Cissette) 925.00
    8" hp., BK, 1970–1972 (Wendy Ann) 145.00
    8" hp., straight leg, 1973–1975, marked "Alex." (Wendy Ann) 60.00
    8" hp., straight leg, 1976–1989, marked "Alexander" (Wendy Ann) (1985-1987 white face) 55.00
    8" reintroduced, 1991 only (Wendy Ann) 55.00
DESERT STORM (see "Welcome Home")
DICKINSON, EMILY 14", 1989 only, Classic Series (Mary Ann) 90.00
DICKSIE & DUCKSIE Cloth/felt, 1930's 600.00
DILLY DALLY SALLY 7" compo., 1937–1942 (Tiny Betty) 275.00
    9" compo., 1938–1939 (Little Betty) 300.00
DING DONG DELL 7" compo., 1937–1942 (Tiny Betty) 285.00
DINNER AT EIGHT 10", 1989–1991, Portrette Series (Cissette) 58.00–60.00
DIONNE QUINTS Original mint or very slight craze.

20" compo. toddlers, 1938–1939	725.00 each	4,300.00 set
19" compo. toddlers, 1936–1938	700.00 each	4,200.00 set
16–17" compo. toddlers, 1937–1939	625.00 each	3,600.00 set
14" compo. toddlers, 1937–1938	425.00 each	2,450.00 set
11" compo. toddlers, wigs & sleep eyes, 1937–1938	350.00 each	2,000.00 set
11" compo. toddlers, molded hair & sleep eyes, 1937–1938	350.00 each	2,000.00 set
11" compo. babies, wigs & sleep eyes, 1936	300.00 each	2,000.00 set
11" compo. babies, molded hair & sleep eyes, 1936	300.00 each	2,000.00 set
8" compo. toddlers, molded hair & painted eyes, 1935–1939	175.00 each	1,200.00 set
8" compo. toddlers, wigs and painted eyes, 1935–1939	175.00 each	1,200.00 set
14" cloth body/compo., 1938	500.00 each	3,200.00 set
17" cloth body/compo., 1938	550.00 each	3,500.00 set
22" cloth/compo., 1936–1937		675.00
24" all cloth, 1935–1936		900.00
16" all cloth, 1935–1936		700.00 up

DISNEY (see Special Events/Exclusives)

DOLL FINDERS (see Special Events/Exclusives)

DOLLS OF THE MONTH 7–8" compo., 1936–1938 (Tiny Betty) 245.00

DOLLS 'N BEARLAND (see Special Events/Exclusives)

DOLLY 8", 1988–1989, Storybook Series (Wendy Ann) 90.00

DOLLY DEARS (see Special Events/Exclusives)

DOLLY DRYPER 11" vinyl, 1952 only, 7 pc. layette 80.00

DOMINICAN REPUBLIC 8" straight leg, 1986–1988 (1985–1986 white face) 60.00

DOROTHY 14", 1990–1992, all blue/white check dress (Mary Ann) 84.00

    8" hp., 1991–1992 (Wendy Ann)..52.00

DOTTIE DUMBUNNIE Cloth/felt, 1930's 900.00

DRESSED FOR OPERA 18" hp., 1953 only (Margaret)..1,200.00

DRUM MAJORETTE 7½" hp., 1955 only (Wendy Ann)..900.00

DUDE RANCH 8" hp., 1955 only (Wendy Ann) 700.00

DUMPLIN' BABY 20–23½", 1957–1958 ....250.00

DUTCH 7" compo., 1935–1939 (Tiny Betty) 245.00

    9" compo boy or girl, 1936–1941 ....275.00

    8" hp. boy*, BKW, 1964 (Wendy Ann) 175.00

    BK, 1965–1972 ....145.00

    8" hp., straight leg, 1972–1973, marked "Alex." 60.00

    8" hp. girl*, BKW, 1961–1964 ....175.00

    8" hp. BK, 1965–1972 ....60.00

    8" BKW, 1964 only (Maggie Mixup) 200.00

* *Both became* NETHERLAND *in 1974.*

14" EMILY DICKINSON

20" DIONNE QUINT holds child's Dionne purse with picture of quints on the clasp.

Please read "About Pricing" for additional information.

EASTER DOLL   8" hp., 1968 only (Wendy Ann) 1,000.00
    14" plastic/vinyl, 1968 only (Mary Ann) 950.00
EASTER BONNET   14", 1992 (Louisa/Jennifer) 145.00
EASTER BUNNY   8", 1990 (see Child at Heart under Special Events/Exclusives)
ECUADOR   8" hp., BK & BKW, 1963–1966 (Wendy Ann) 350.00
EDITH, THE LONELY DOLL   16" plastic/vinyl, 1958–1959 ....245.00
    22", 1958–1959 ....325.00
    8" hp., 1958 only (Wendy Ann) 600.00
EDITH WITH GOLDEN HAIR   18" cloth, 1940's 600.00
EDWARDIAN   18" hp., 1953 only, Glamour Girl Series (Margaret) 1,200.00
    8" hp., 1953 only (Wendy Ann) 950.00
EISENHOWER, MAMIE   14", 6th set Presidents' Ladies/First Ladies Series, 1989–1990 (Mary Ann).......100.00
EGYPT   8" straight leg, 1986–1989 (Wendy Ann) 90.00
EGYPTIAN   7–8" compo., 1936–1940 (Tiny Betty) 285.00
    9" compo., 1936–1940 (Little Betty) 300.00
ELAINE   18" hp., 1954 only, blue organdy dress, Me & My Shadow Series (Cissy) 1,300.00
    8" hp., 1954 only, matches 18" (Wendy Ann) 1,100.00
ELISE   16½" hp./vinyl arms., jointed ankles & knees, 1957–1964 (18", 1963 only)
    In street clothes 125.00
    In ballgown 275.00
    Ballerina 185.00
    With Marybel head, 1962 only 225.00

17" ELISE BALLERINA, 1970

18" with bouffant hairstyle, 1963 only 250.00
14" plastic/vinyl, 1988 only 75.00
17" hp./vinyl one–piece arms & legs, jointed ankles & knees, 1961–1962 ....200.00
18" hp./vinyl, jointed ankles & knees, 1963–1964 ....200.00
In riding habit 350.00
17" plastic/vinyl, street dress – 1966 only 200.00
17" in trunk/trousseau, 1966–1972 ....750.00 up
17" Portrait, 1972–1973 ....200.00
17" in formal, 1966, 1976–1977 ....200.00
17" Bride, 1966–1987 ....100.00
17" Ballerina, 1966–1991 ....65.00–125.00
17" Elise in any discontinued costume, 1966–1989 ....100.00
ELIZA 14", Classic Series, 1991 only (Louisa) 155.00
EMILY Cloth/felt, 1930's 600.00
EMPRESS ELIZABETH 1991 (see My Doll House under Special Events/Exclusives)
ENCHANTED DOLL (see Special Events/Exclusives)
ENCHANTED EVENING 21" Portrait, 1991, different necklace than shown in catalog (Cissy) 280.00
ENGLISH GUARD 8" hp., BK, 1966–1968, Portrait Children Series (Wendy Ann) 550.00
8" reintroduced 1989–1991, marked "Alexander" (Wendy Ann)...55.00
ESKIMO 8" hp., BK, 1967–1969, Americana Series (Wendy Ann) 475.00
9" compo., 1936–1939 (Little Betty) 265.00
With Maggie Mixup face 500.00
ESTONIA 8" straight leg, 1986–1987 only (Wendy Ann) 90.00
EVA LOVELACE 7" compo., 1935 only (Tiny Betty) 245.00
Cloth, 1935 only 600.00
EVANGELINE 18" cloth, 1930's 700.00

ENCHANTED DOLL, 1980

Please read "About Pricing" for additional information.

F.A.O. Schwarz (see Special Events/Exclusives)

Fairy Godmother 14", 1983–1992, Classic Series (Mary Ann, Louisa) 100.00–165.00
    Fairy outfit, 1983, M.A.D.C. (see Special Events/Exclusives)

Fairy Princess 7–8" compo., 1940–1943 (Tiny Betty) 285.00
    9" compo., 1939–1941 (Little Betty) 300.00
    11" compo., 1939 only (Wendy Ann)...350.00
    15–18" compo., 1939–1942 (Wendy Ann)...600.00–700.00
    21–22" compo., 1939, 1944–1946 (Wendy Ann) 950.00

Fairy Queen 14½" compo., 1940–1946 (Wendy Ann)..600.00
    18" compo., 1940–1946 (Wendy Ann) 750.00
    18" hp., 1949–1950 (Margaret) 885.00
    14½" hp., 1948–1950 (Margaret) 675.00

Fairy Tales – Dumas 9" compo., 1937–1941 (Little Betty) 300.00

Faith 8" hp., Americana Group, 1961 only, (Wendy Ann) ....2,100.00 up
    8" hp. (see C.U. under Special Events/Exclusives)

Fantasy 8", 1990 (see Doll Finders under Special Events/Exclusives)

14" Fairy Godmother, 1992

FANNIE ELIZABETH 8" (see Belks under Special Events/Exclusives)
FARMER'S DAUGHTER Enchanted Doll House, 1991 (see Special Events/Exclusives)
FASHIONS OF THE CENTURY 14–18" hp., 1954–1955 (Margaret, Maggie)................................1,100.00
FILLMORE, ABIGAIL 1982–1984, 3rd set Presidents' Ladies/First Ladies Series (Louisa) 95.00
FINDLAY, JANE 1979–1981, 1st set Presidents' Ladies/First Ladies Series (Mary Ann) 120.00
FINLAND 8" hp., BK, 1968–1972 (Wendy Ann) 125.00
    8" hp., straight leg, 1973–1975, marked "Alex." 60.00
    8" hp., straight leg, 1976–1987, marked "Alexander" (1985–1987 white face) 55.00
FINNISH 7" compo., 1935–1937 (Tiny Betty)..245.00
FIRST COMMUNION 8" hp., 1957 only (Wendy Ann) 750.00
    14", Classics Series, 1991–1992 (Louisa) 95.00
FIRST LADIES (see "Presidents' Ladies")
FIRST MODERN DOLL CLUB (see Special Events/Exclusives)
FISHER QUINTS 7" hp./vinyl, 1964 only (Little Genius) 400.00
FIVE LITTLE PEPPERS 13" & 16" compo, 1936 only..each 500.00–600.00
FLAPPER 10", Portrette Series, 1988–1991 (Cissette) 65.00
    10", 1988 (see under M.A.D.C. in Special Events/Exclusives)
FLORA MCFLIMSEY (with and without "e").
    9" compo., 1938–1941 (Little Betty) 300.00
    22" compo., 1938–1944 (Princess Elizabeth)..700.00
    15–16" compo., 1938–1944 (Princess Elizabeth)...500.00
    16–17" compo., 1936–1937 (Wendy Ann) 500.00
    14" compo., 1938–1944 (Princess Elizabeth)..450.00
    12" compo., 1944 only, holds 5" "Nancy Ann" doll, tagged "Margie Ann" (Wendy Ann) 600.00
    15" Miss Flora McFlimsey, vinyl head, 1953 only (Cissy) 575.00
FLOWERGIRL 16"–18" compo., 1939, 1944–1947 (Princess Elizabeth)..550.00
    20–24" compo., 1939, 1944–1947 (Princess Elizabeth) 750.00
    15–18" hp., 1954 only (Cissy) 425.00
    15" hp., 1954 only (Margaret)...600.00
    8" hp., 1956 (Wendy Ann)..650.00
    8" hp., 1992, Americana Series, black or white doll (Wendy Ann) 55.00
    10", 1988–1990, Portrette Series (Cissette)...70.00
FRANCE 7" compo., 1936–1943 (Tiny Betty) 265.00
FRENCH 9" compo., 1937–1941 (Little Betty) 265.00
    8" hp., BKW, 1961–1965 (Wendy Ann) 150.00
    8" hp., BK, 1965–1972 ....135.00
    8" hp., straight leg, 1973–1975, marked "Alex." 60.00
    8" straight leg, 1976–1992, marked "Alexander" (1985–1987 white face) 52.00
    1985 white face 55.00
FRENCH ARISTOCRAT 10" Portrette, 1991 (Cissette)...105.00
FRENCH FLOWERGIRL 8" hp., 1956 only (Wendy Ann)...650.00
FRIAR TUCK 8" hp., 1989–1991 (Maggie Mixup)...65.00
FRIEDRICH (see "Sound of Music")
FROU-FROU 40" all cloth, yarn hair, 1951 only, ballerina in green, lilac 700.00
FUNNY 18" cloth, 1963–1977 ....50.00

Please read "About Pricing" for additional information.

GAINSBOROUGH 20" hp., 1957, taffeta gown, large picture hat, Models Formals Series (Cissy) 1,000.00
     #2184, 21" hp./vinyl arms, 1968, blue with white lace jacket (Jacqueline) 650.00
     #2192, 21", 1972, yellow with full white overlace (Jacqueline) 550.00
     #2192, 21", 1973, pale blue, scallop lace overskirt (Jacqueline) 475.00
     #2211, 21", 1978, pink with full lace overdress (Jacqueline) 350.00
         10" (Cissette) 425.00
GARDEN PARTY 18" hp., 1953 only (Margaret) 1,400.00
     20" hp., 1956–1957 (Cissy) 875.00
     8" hp., 1955 only (Wendy Ann) 1,200.00
GARFIELD, LUCRETIA 1985–1987, 4th set Presidents' Ladies/First Ladies Series (Louisa) 90.00
GENIUS BABY 21"–30" plastic/vinyl, flirty eyes, 1960–1961 .... 100.00–150.00
     Little, 8" hp. head/vinyl, 1956–1962 (see Little Genius)
GERANIUM 9" early vinyl toddler, 1953 only, red organdy dress & bonnet .... 95.00 up
GERMAN (GERMANY) 8" hp., BK, 1966–1972 (Wendy Ann) 135.00
     8" hp., straight leg, 1973–1975, marked "Alex." 60.00
     10" hp., 1962–1963 (Cissette) 1,250.00
     8" straight legs, 1976–1991, marked "Alexander" (1985–1987 white face) 55.00
     8" white face, 1986 .... 55.00
GIBSON GIRL 10" hp., 1962, eye shadow (Cissette) 750.00
     1963, plain blouse with no stripes 600.00
     16" cloth, 1930's 775.00
     10", 1988–1990, Portrette Series (Cissette) 75.00
GIDGET 14" plastic/vinyl, 1966 only (Mary Ann) 325.00
GIGI 14", 1986–1987, Classic Series (Mary Ann) 75.00

14" GIGI, 1987

GIRL ON FLYING TRAPEZE 40" cloth, 1951 only, dressed in pink satin tutu 750.00
GLAMOUR GIRLS 18" hp., 1953 only (Margaret, Maggie) 1,250.00
GLENDA, THE GOOD WITCH 8", 1992, Storyland Series (Wendy Ann) 60.00
GODEY 21" compo., 1945–1947 (Wendy Ann) 1,600.00
    14" hp., 1950–1951 (Margaret) 1,200.00
    20" hp., 1951 only (Margaret) 1,500.00
    18" hp., 1953 only, Glamour Girl Series (Maggie) 1,300.00
    21" hp., vinyl straight arms, 1961 only (Cissy) 1,200.00
    #2153, 21", 1965, dressed in all red, blonde hair (Jacqueline) 625.00
    #2172, 21" hp., vinyl arms, 1967, dressed in pink & ecru (Jacqueline) 575.00
    #2195, 1969, red with black trim 475.00
    #2195, 1970, pink with burgundy short jacket 325.00
    #2161, 1971, pink, black trim, short jacket 350.00
    #2298, 1977, ecru with red jacket and bonnet 325.00
    8" SLW, 1955 only (Wendy Ann) 1,200.00
    10" hp., 1968, dressed in all pink with bows down front (Cissette) 500.00
        1969, all yellow with bows down front 500.00
        1970, all lace pink dress with natural straw hat 750.00
    21" plastic/vinyl, 1966 only, red with black short jacket & hat (Coco) 2,400.00

21" GODEY, 1961

GODEY BRIDE   14" hp., 1950 (Margaret) 875.00
    18" hp., 1950–1951 (Margaret) 950.00
GODEY GROOM/MAN   14" hp., 1950 (Margaret) 900.00
    18" hp., 1950–1951 (Margaret) 1,100.00
GODEY LADY   14" hp., 1950 (Margaret) 950.00
    18" hp., 1950–1951 (Margaret) 1,200.00
GOLD RUSH   10" hp., 1963 only (Cissette) 1,200.00
GOLDILOCKS   18" cloth, 1930's 750.00
    7–8" compo., 1938–1942 (Tiny Betty) 275.00
    18" hp., 1951 only (Maggie) 950.00
    14" plastic/vinyl, 1978–1979, Classic Series, satin dress (Mary Ann) 75.00
    14", 1980–1983, cotton dress (Mary Ann) 75.00
    14", Classic Series, 1991 only, long side curls tied with ribbon (Mary Ann) 95.00
    8", 1990–1991 only, Storyland Series (1991 dress in different plaid) (Wendy Ann) 55.00
GONE WITH THE WIND (SCARLETT)   14", 1968–1986, all white dress/green sash (Mary Ann) 90.00
GOOD FAIRY   14" hp. (Margaret) 675.00
GOOD LITTLE GIRL   16" cloth, 1966 only, wears pink dress, mate to "Bad Little Girl" 90.00
GOYA   8" hp., 1953 only (Wendy Ann) 1,200.00
    #2183, 21" hp./vinyl arms, 1968, multi–tier pink dress (Jacqueline) 550.00
    #2235, 21", 1982–1983, maroon dress with black Spanish lace (Jacqueline) 250.00
GRADUATION   8" hp., 1957 only (Wendy Ann) 1,250.00
    12", 1957 only (Lissy) 900.00
    8", 1990–1992, Americana Series (white doll only) (Wendy Ann) 55.00
    8", 1991–1992, white or black doll 55.00
GRANDMA JANE   14" plastic/vinyl, 1970–1972 (Mary Ann) 265.00
GRANT, JULIA   1982–1984, 3rd set First Ladies/Presidents' Ladies Series (Louisa) 95.00
GRAVE, ALICE   18" cloth, 1930's 650.00
GRAYSON, KATHRYN   20–21" hp., 1949 only (Margaret) 2,400.00
GREAT BRITAIN   8" hp., 1977–1988 (Wendy Ann) (1985–1987 white face) 55.00
GREECE BOY   8" hp., 1992 (Wendy Ann) 52.00
GREEK BOY   8" hp., BK & BKW, 1965–1968 (Wendy Ann) 325.00
GREEK GIRL   8" hp., BK, 1968–1972 (Wendy Ann) 135.00
    8" hp., straight leg, 1973–1975, marked "Alex." 60.00
    8" hp., straight leg, 1976–1987, marked "Alexander" (1985–1987 white face) 55.00
GRETEL   7" compo., 1935–1942 (Tiny Betty) 275.00
    9" compo., 1938–1940 (Little Betty) 300.00
    18" hp., 1948 only (Margaret) 975.00
    7½–8" hp., SLW, 1955 (Wendy Ann) 750.00
    8" hp., BK, 1966–1972, Storybook Series (Wendy Ann) 135.00
    8" hp., straight leg, 1973–1975, marked "Alex." 60.00
    8" hp., straight leg, 1976–1986, marked "Alexander" (1986 white face) 55.00
    8" hp., reintroduced, Storyland Series (Wendy Ann) 50.00
GRETL   (see "Sound of Music")
GROOM   18" – 21" compo., 1946–1947 (Margaret) 900.00
    18–21" hp., 1949–1951 (Margaret) 850.00
    14–16" hp., 1949–1951 (Margaret) 600.00
    7½" hp., 1953–1955 (Wendy Ann) 425.00
    8" hp., 1961–1963 (Wendy Ann) 350.00
    8", reintroduced 1989–1991 only (Wendy Ann) 60.00
GUENIVERE   10", 1992, Portrette Series 95.00

Please read "About Pricing" for additional information.

HALLOWEEN WITCH 8" C.U. (see Special Events/Exclusives)
HAMLET 12", Romance Collection (Nancy Drew) 95.00
HANSEL 7" compo., 1935–1942 (Tiny Betty) 285.00
   9" compo., 1938–1940 (Little Betty) 300.00
   18" hp., 1948 only (Margaret)..675.00
   8" hp., SLW, 1955 only (Wendy Ann)..500.00
   8" hp., BK, 1966–1972, Storybook Series (Wendy Ann)..135.00
   8" hp., straight leg, 1973–1975, marked "Alex." 60.00
   8" hp., straight leg, 1976–1986, marked "Alexander" (1986 white face) 55.00
   8" hp., reintroduced, 1991–1992, Storyland Series (Wendy Ann)..52.00
HAPPY 20" cloth/vinyl, 1970 only..250.00
HAPPY BIRTHDAY M.A.D.C., 1985 (see Special Events/Exclusives)
   8" hp., Americana Series, black or white doll (Wendy Ann)..50.00
HARDING, FLORENCE 1988, 5th set Presidents' Ladies/First Ladies Series (Louisa) 85.00
HARRISON, CAROLINE 1985–1987, 4th set Presidents' Ladies/First Ladies Series (Louisa) 90.00
HAWAII 8", 1990–1991 only, Americana Series, (Wendy Ann)..55.00
HAWAIIAN 8" hp., BK, 1966–1969, Americana Series (Wendy Ann) 425.00
   7" compo., 1936–1939 (Tiny Betty) 285.00
   9" compo., 1937–1944 (Little Betty) 325.00
HAYES, LUCY 1985–1987, 4th set Presidents' Ladies/First Ladies Series (Louisa) 90.00
HEATHER 18" cloth/vinyl, 1990 to date 85.00

14" LUCY HAYES
Presidents' Ladies, 4th set, 1985–1987

SONJA HENIE
using the Madeline doll

HEIDI 7" compo., 1938–1939 (Tiny Betty) 275.00
    14" plastic/vinyl, 1969–1988, Classic Series (Mary Ann) 75.00
    8" hp., 1991–1992, Storyland Series (Maggie) 55.00
HELLO BABY 22", 1962 only 145.00
HENIE, SONJA 13–15" compo., 1939–1942 ....575.00
    7" compo., 1939–1942 (Tiny Betty) 300.00
    9" compo., 1940–1941 (Little Betty) 400.00
    11" compo. (Wendy Ann) 500.00
    14" compo. 575.00
    14" in case/wardrobe ....1,000.00 up
    17–18" compo. 900.00
    20–23" compo. 1,000.00
    13–14" compo., jointed waist 800.00
    15–18" hp./vinyl, no extra joints, 1951 only (Madeline) 1,000.00
HIAWATHA 8" hp., 1967–1969, Americana Series (Wendy Ann) 365.00
    7" compo. (Tiny Betty) 285.00
    18" cloth, early 1930's 650.00
HIGHLAND FLING 8" hp., 1955 only (Wendy Ann) 575.00

HIGHLAND FLING, 1955

HILDA 18" compo., black doll, 1947 only (Margaret)..1,200.00 up
HOLIDAY ON ICE 8" hp., 1992 (Wendy Ann)..55.00
HOLLAND 7" compo., 1936–1943 (Tiny Betty)...245.00
HOLLY 10", 1990–1991, Portrette Series (Cissette) 85.00
HONEYBEA 12" vinyl, 1963 only...125.00

HONEYETTE BABY 16" compo./cloth, 1941–1942 ....125.00
  7" compo., 1934–1937, little girl dress (Tiny Betty) 175.00
HONEYBUN 18–19", 1951–1952 only 140.00
  23–26" 175.00
HOOVER, LOU 14", 1989–1990, 6th set First Ladies/Presidents' Ladies Series (Mary Ann) 100.00
HUCKLEBERRY FINN 8" hp., 1989–1991 only, Storybook Series (Wendy Ann) 60.00
HULDA 18" compo., 1946 only (Margaret) ....1,000.00 up
HUGGUMS, LITTLE 14", molded hair, 1986 only 50.00
  12" molded hair. 1963–1992 ....55.00
  12" rooted hair, 1963–1982, 1988 ....55.00
  1991, special outfits for Imaginarium Shop (see Special Events/Exclusives)
HUGGUMS, BIG 25", 1963–1979, boy or girl 95.00
  Lively, 25", 1963 only, knob moves head and limbs 125.00
HUNGARIAN (HUNGARY) 8" hp., BKW, 1962–1965 (Wendy Ann) 175.00
  BK with metal crown 150.00
  BK, 1965–1972 ....135.00
  8" hp., straight leg, 1973–1976, marked "Alex." 60.00
  8" hp., straight leg, 1976–1986, marked "Alexander" (1986 white face) 55.00
  8" hp., reintroduced 1992 (Wendy Ann) 50.00
HYACINTH 9" early vinyl toddler, 1953 only, blue dress & bonnet ....95.00 up

14" HONOR, 1988

Please read "About Pricing" for additional information.

IBIZA 8", 1989 only (Wendy Ann) 90.00
ICE CAPADES 1950's (Cissy) ....1,200.00 up
  1960's (Jacqueline) ....1,500.00 up
ICE SKATER 8" hp., BK & BKW, 1955–1956 (Wendy Ann) ....550.00 up
  8", 1990–1991 only, Americana Series (Wendy Ann) 60.00
ICELAND 10", 1962–1963 (Cissette) 1,200.00
IMAGINARIUM SHOP (see Special Events/Exclusives)
I. MAGNIN STORE (see Special Events/Exclusives)
INDIA 8" hp., BKW, 1965 (Wendy Ann) 275.00
  8" hp., BK, 1965–1972 (Wendy Ann) 135.00
  8" hp., BK & BKW, white 135.00
  8" hp., straight leg, 1973–1975, marked "Alex." 60.00
  8" hp., straight leg, 1976–1988, marked "Alexander" (1985–1987 white face) 55.00
  10" hp., 1962–1963 (Cissette) ....1,200.00 up
INDIAN BOY 8" hp., BK, 1966 only, Americana Series (Wendy Ann) 365.00
INDIAN GIRL 8" hp., BK, 1966 only, Americana Series (Wendy Ann) 400.00

8" INDIAN BOY AND GIRL, 1966

INDONESIA 8" hp., BK, 1970–1972 (Wendy Ann) 200.00
  8" hp., straight leg, 1972–1975, marked "Alex." 60.00
  8" hp., straight leg, 1976–1988, marked "Alexander" 55.00
  With Maggie Mixup face, BK 250.00
INGALLS, LAURA 14", 1989–1991, Classic Series (Mary Ann) 85.00
INGRES 14" plastic/vinyl, 1987 only, Fine Arts Series (Mary Ann) 75.00
IRIS 10" hp., 1987–1988 (Cissette) 75.00
IRISH (IRELAND) 8" hp., BKW, 1965 only (Wendy Ann) 185.00
  8" BK, 1966–1972, long gown 135.00
  8" straight leg, 1973–1975, marked "ALEX", long gown 60.00
  8" straight leg, 1976–1985, marked "Alexander" 55.00
  8" straight leg, 1985–1987, short dress, white face 55.00
  8" straight leg, 1987–1992, marked "Alexander," short dress (Maggie) 50.00

ISOLDE 14", 1985–1986 only, Opera Series (Mary Ann) 90.00
ISRAEL 8" hp., BK, 1965–1972 (Wendy Ann) 135.00
    8" hp., straight leg, 1973–1975, marked "Alex." 60.00
    8" hp., straight leg, 1976–1989, marked "Alexander" (1985–1987 white face) 55.00
ITALY 8" hp., BKW, 1961–1965 (Wendy Ann) 175.00
    8" hp., BK, 1965–1972 .... 135.00
    8" hp., straight leg, 1973–1975, marked "ALEX." 60.00
    1985 white face 55.00
    8" straight leg, 1976–1992, marked "Alexander" 55.00

14" ISOLDE, 1985

Please read "About Pricing" for additional information.

JACK & JILL   7" compo., 1938–1943 (Tiny Betty) ....each 285.00
    9" compo., 1939 only (Little Betty)...each 300.00
    8" straight leg, 1987–1992, Storybook Series (Maggie) ....each 52.00
JACKSON, SARAH   1979–1981, 2nd set Presidents' Ladies/First Ladies Series (Louisa) 105.00
JACQUELINE IN RIDING HABIT   1962 ....575.00
    In gown from cover of 1962 catalog 700.00
JACQUELINE   21" hp./vinyl arms, 1961–1962, street dress or suit 575.00
    Ballgown 700.00
    10" hp., 1962 only (Cissette) 475.00
JACQUELINE   1962, 1966–1967, exclusive in trunk with wardrobe ....1,400.00 up
JAMAICA   8" straight leg, 1986–1988 (Wendy Ann) 75.00
JANIE   12" toddler, 1964–1966 only 285.00
    Ballerina, 1965 only 300.00
    14" baby, 1972–1973 ....70.00
    20" baby, 1972–1973 ....90.00
JAPAN   8" hp., BK, 1968–1972 (Wendy Ann)...135.00
    8" hp., straight leg, 1973–1975, marked "Alex." 60.00

21" JACQUELINE, 1961–1962

8" hp., straight leg, 1976–1986, marked "Alexander" 55.00
8", 1987–1991 (Maggie) 55.00
8" BK, 1960's (Maggie Mixup) 155.00
8" hp., reintroduced 1992, white face (Wendy Ann) 60.00
JASMINE 10", 1987–1988, Portrette Series (Cissette) 75.00
JEANNIE WALKER 13–14" compo., 1940's 500.00
  18" compo., 1940's 675.00
JENNIFER'S TRUNK SET 14" doll, 1990 only 245.00
JESSICA 18" cloth/vinyl, 1990 only 145.00
JO (see Little Women)
JOANIE 36" plastic/vinyl, 1960–1961 .... 350.00
  36" Nurse, 1960, all white with black band on cap 385.00
  36" Nurse, 1961, colored dress, all white pinafore and cap 385.00
JOHN POWER'S MODELS 14" hp., 1952 only (Maggie & Margaret) 1,200.00
  18", 1952 only 1,300.00
JONES, CASEY 8" hp., Americana Series, 1991 (Wendy Ann) 52.00
JOSEPHINE 12", 1980–1986, Portrait of History (Nancy Drew) 75.00
JOY 12", 1990, New England Collectors (see Special Events/Exclusives)
JUDY 21" compo., 1945–1947 (Wendy Ann) .... 2,300.00 up
  21" hp./vinyl arms, 1962 only (Jacqueline) 1,700.00
JUGO-SLAV 7" compo., 1935–1937 (Tiny Betty) 265.00
JULIET 21" compo., 1945–1946, Portrait Series (Wendy Ann) 2,300.00
  18" compo., 1937–1940 (Wendy Ann) 1,200.00
  8" hp., 1955 only (Wendy Ann) 1,300.00
  12" plastic/vinyl, 1978–1987, Portrait Children Series (Nancy Drew) 75.00
  12", reintroduced 1991–1992, Romance Collection (Nancy Drew) 105.00
JUNE BRIDE 21" compo., 1939, 1946–1947, Portrait Series 1,900.00
JUNE WEDDING 8" hp., 1956 only (Wendy Ann) 750.00

Please read "About Pricing" for additional information.

KAREN 15–18" hp., 1948–1949 (Margaret) 875.00
KAREN BALLERINA 15" compo., 1947–1949 (Margaret) 700.00
   18–21" 750.00
KATE GREENAWAY 7" compo., 1938–1943 (Tiny Betty)..285.00
   9" comp., 1936–1939 (Little Betty) 325.00
   16" cloth, 1936–1938 ....900.00
   13", 14", 15" compo., 1938–1943 (Princess Elizabeth) 475.00–600.00
   18", 1938–1943 ....700.00
   24", 1938–1943 ....850.00
KATHLEEN TODDLER 23" rigid vinyl, 1959 only 125.00
KATIE (BLACK SMARTY) 12" plastic/vinyl, 1963 only 350.00
   12" (Black Janie) 1965 only 325.00
   12" hp., 1962 Anniversary doll for FAO Schwarz (Lissy) 1,200.00
KATHY 15–18" hp., 1949–1951, has braids (Maggie)...900.00
KATHY BABY 13–15" vinyl, rooted or molded hair, 1954–1956 ....65.00–125.00
   11–13" vinyl, rooted or molded hair, 1955–1956 ....65.00–125.00
   18–21", rooted or molded hair, 1954–1956 ....100.00–150.00
   11" vinyl, molded hair, 1955–1956, has trousseau 125.00
   21", 1954 only 165.00
   21" & 25", 1955–1956 ....125.00–200.00
KATHY CRY DOLLY 11–15" vinyl, nurser, 1957–1958 ....60.00–85.00
   18", 21", 25" 75.00–125.00

8" KATHY, 1954–1956

Kathy Tears 11", 15", 17" vinyl, closed mouth 1959–1962 ....50.00–85.00
    19", 23", 26", 1959–1962 ....100.00–150.00
    12", 16", 19" vinyl, 1960–1961 (New face) 60.00–85.00
Keane, Doris Cloth, 1930's 800.00
    9–11" compo., 1936–1937 (Little Betty) 285.00
Kelly 12" hp., 1959 only (Lissy) 425.00
    15–16", 1958–1959 (Marybel)..300.00
    16" in trunk/wardrobe, 1959 only 485.00
    22", 1958–1959 ....450.00
Kennedy, Jacqueline 14", 1989–1990, 6th set Presidents' Ladies/First Ladies Series (Mary Ann).......90.00
King 21" compo., 1942–1946 (Wendy Ann)..2,300.00
Kitten 14–18" cloth/vinyl, 1962–1963 ....35.00–75.00
    24", rooted hair, 1961 only..85.00
    20", nurser, doesn't wet, cryer box, 1968 only 75.00
    20", 1985–1986 only, dressed in pink 85.00
Kitten Kries 20" cloth/vinyl, 1967 only...85.00
Kitten, Mama 18", 1963 only, same as "Lively" but also has cryer box.............................100.00
Kitten, Lively 14", 18", 24", knob moves head and limbs, 1962–1963 ....100.00
Kitty Baby 21" compo., 1941–1942 ....125.00
Klondike Kate 10" hp., 1963 only, Portrette Series (Cissette) 1,000.00
Korea 8" hp., BK, 1968–1970 (Wendy Ann)..450.00
    BKW & BK (Maggie Mixup)..500.00
    Reintroduced 1988–1989 (Maggie Mixup) 90.00

8" Kelly, 1959 (Alexanderkin)

Please read "About Pricing" for additional information.

LADY BIRD 8", 1988–1989, Storybook Series (Maggie) 90.00
LADY HAMILTON 20" hp./vinyl arms, 1957 only, picture hat, blue gown w/shoulder shawl effect,
  Models Formal Series (Cissy) 750.00
    11" hp., 1957, pink silk gown, picture hat with roses (Cissette) 425.00
    #2182, 21", 1968, beige lace over pink gown (Jacqueline) 475.00
    12" vinyl, 1984–1986, Portrait of History (Nancy Drew) 55.00
LADY IN RED 20", 1958 only, red taffeta (Cissy) 1,200.00
    10", 1990, Portrette Series (Cissette) 75.00
LADY IN WAITING 8" hp., 1955 only (Wendy Ann) 1,400.00
LADY LEE 8", 1988 only, Storybook Series 90.00
LADY LOVELACE Cloth/felt, 1930's 600.00
LADY WINDERMERE 21" compo., 1945–1946 .... 2,300.00
LAMARR, HEDY 17" hp., 1949 only (Margaret) .... 1,200.00 up
LANE, HARRIET 1982–1984, 3rd set Presidents' Ladies/First Ladies Series (Mary Ann) 95.00
LAOS 8" straight leg, 1987–1988 .... 75.00
LATVIA 8" straight leg, 1987 only 75.00
LAUGHING ALLEGRA Cloth, 1932 .... 700.00
LAURIE, LITTLE MEN 8" hp., BK, 1966–1972 (Wendy Ann) 135.00
    Straight leg, 1973–1975, marked "Alex." 60.00
    Check pants, marked "Alexander" 55.00
    Straight leg, 1976–1992 (1985–1987 white face) 50.00
    12" all hp., 1967–1968 (Lissy) 325.00
    12" plastic/vinyl, 1967–1988 (Nancy Drew) 75.00

17" LESLIE, 1965–1971

LAURIE, PIPER 14" hp., 1950 only (Margaret) ....1,200.00 up
    21" hp., 1950 only ....1,400.00 up
LAZY MARY 7" compo., 1936–1938 (Tiny Betty) 275.00
LENA (see "River Boat")
LESLIE (BLACK POLLY) 17" vinyl, 1965–1971, in dress 375.00
    Bride, 1966–1971 ....300.00
    In formal, 1965–1971 ....465.00
    In trunk/wardrobe ....800.00 up
    Ballerina, 1966–1971 ....350.00
LETTY BRIDESMAID 7–8" compo., 1938–1940 (Tiny Betty) 275.00
LEWIS, SHARI 14", 1958–1959 ....300.00
    21", 1958–1959 ....475.00
LIESL (see "Sound of Music")
LILA BRIDESMAID 7–8" compo., 1938–1940 (Tiny Betty) 265.00
LILIBET 16" compo., 1938 (Princess Elizabeth) 750.00
LILY 10", 1987–1988 (Cissette) 75.00
LINCOLN, MARY TODD 1982–1984, 3rd set Presidents' Ladies/First Ladies Series (Louisa) 275.00
LIND, JENNY #2191, 21" hp./vinyl arms, 1969, dressed in all pink, no trim (Jacqueline)...............1,700.00
    #2181, 1970, all pink with lace trim 1,700.00
    10", 1969, Portrette Series, all pink, no trim (Cissette) 650.00
    10", 1970, Portrette Series, pink with lace trim (Cissette) 650.00
    14" plastic/vinyl, 1970–1971, Portrait Children Series (Mary Ann) 385.00
LIND, JENNY & LISTENING CAT 1970–1971, Portrait Children Series (Mary Ann) 385.00
LION TAMER 8", 1990, Americana Series (Wendy Ann) 80.00
LISSY 11½"–12" hp., jointed knees & elbows, 1956–1958 ....285.00
    Ballerina, 1956–1958 ....325.00
    Bride, 1956–1958 ....300.00
    Bridesmaid, 1956–1957 ....400.00
    Formals, 1958 ....400.00
    Street dresses, 1956–1958 ....285.00
    Window box with wardrobe, 1956 ....1,200.00 up
    21", one-piece arm, pink tulle pleated skirt (Cissy) 950.00
    #2051, 21", pink tiara, 1966 (Coco) 2,200.00
    12" hp., jointed elbows & knees, in window box/wardrobe, 1957 (Lissy) ....950.00 up
    12" hp., one-piece arms & legs in window box/wardrobe, 1959–1966 (Lissy) ....750.00 up
    Classics (see individuals, example: McGuffey Ana, Scarlett, Cinderella)
LITTLE ANGEL 9" latex/vinyl, 1950–1957 ....145.00
LITTLE AUDREY Vinyl, 1954 only 200.00
LITTLE BETTY 9–11" compo., 1935–1943 ....265.00
LITTLE BITSEY 9" nurser, 1967–1968, all vinyl (Sweet Tears) 165.00
LITTLE BO PEEP (see Bo Peep, Little)
LITTLE BOY BLUE 7" compo., 1937–1939 (Tiny Betty) 275.00
LITTLE BUTCH 9" all vinyl nurser, 1967–1968 (Sweet Tears) 165.00
LITTLE CHERUB 11" compo., 1945–1946 ....165.00
    7" all vinyl, 1960 only 200.00
LITTLE COLONEL 8½–9" compo., closed mouth, 1935 (Betty) 450.00
    11–13" compo., closed mouth (Betty) 575.00–650.00
    14–17", open mouth (Betty) 650.00–675.00
    18–23", open mouth 775.00–850.00
    26–27", open mouth 1,000.00
LITTLE DEVIL 8" hp., Americana Series, 1992 ....55.00
LITTLE DORRIT 16" cloth, Dicken's character, early 1930's 600.00
LITTLE EMILY 16" cloth, Dicken's character, early 1930's 600.00

LITTLE EMPEROR (see U.F.D.C. under Special Events/Exclusives)
LITTLE GENIUS 12–14" compo./cloth, 1935–1940, 1942–1946 ....125.00
   18–20" compo./cloth, 1935–1937, 1942–1946 ....145.00–165.00
   24–25", 1936–1940 ....165.00–185.00
   8" hp./vinyl, 1956–1962, nude (clean condition), good face color 225.00
     Cotton play dress 225.00
     Dressy, lacy outfit with bonnet 300.00
     Christening outfit 385.00
   Sewing or Gift Set, 1950's ....800.00 up
LITTLE GODEY 8" hp., 1953–1955 (Wendy Ann) 1,100.00
LITTLE GRANNY 14" plastic/vinyl, 1966 only (Mary Ann) 225.00
   14", 1966 only, pinstripe and floral gown (also variations) (Mary Ann) 225.00
LITTLE JACK HORNER 7" compo., 1937–1943 (Tiny Betty) 265.00
LITTLE JUMPING JOAN 8", 1989–1990, Storybook Series (Maggie Mixup) 90.00
LITTLE LADY DOLL 8" hp., 1960 only, gift set, in mint condition (Maggie Mixup) ...900.00
   8" doll only 325.00
   21" hp., 1949, has braids & Colonial gown (Wendy Ann) 2,000.00
LITTLE LORD FAUNTLEROY Cloth, 1930's 700.00
   13" compo., 1936–1937 (Wendy Ann) 685.00
LITTLE MADELINE 8" hp., 1953–1954 (Madeline) 525.00
LITTLE MAID 8" straight leg, 1987–1988, Storybook Series (Wendy Ann) 90.00
LITTLE MELANIE 8" hp., 1955–1956, (Wendy Ann) 1,200.00
LITTLE MEN 15" hp., 1950–1952 (Margaret & Maggie) ....each 800.00
LITTLE MEN Set with Tommy, Nat & Stuffy ....set 2,900.00
LITTLE MERMAID 10", Portrette Series, 1992 (Cissette) 105.00
LITTLE MINISTER 8" hp., 1957 only (Wendy Ann) ....1,900.00 up
LITTLE MISS 8" hp., 1989–1991 only, Storybook Series (Maggie Mixup) 55.00
LITTLE MISS MAGNIN (see I. Magnin under Special Events/Exclusives)
LITTLE NANNIE ETTICOAT Straight leg, 1986–1988, Storybook Series 90.00
LITTLE NELL 16" cloth, early 1930's, Dickens character 700.00
   14" compo., 1938–1940 (Wendy Ann) 650.00
LITTLE SHAVER 10" cloth, 1940–1944 ....475.00
   7" cloth, 1940–1944 ....485.00
   15" cloth, 1940–1944 ....525.00
   22", 1940–1944 ....550.00 up
   12" plastic/vinyl, painted eyes, 1963–1965 ....200.00
LITTLE SOUTHERN BOY/GIRL 10" latex/vinyl, 1950–1951 ....each 150.00
LITTLE SOUTHERN GIRL 8" hp., 1953 only (Wendy Ann) 975.00
LITTLE VICTORIA 7½"–8", 1953–1954 only (Wendy Ann) 1,300.00
LITTLE WOMEN (Meg, Jo, Amy, Beth)
   16" cloth, 1930–1936 ....each 625.00–700.00
   7" compo., 1935–1944 (Tiny Betty) ....each 275.00
   9" compo., 1937–1940 (Little Betty) ....each 295.00
   13–15" compo., 1937–1946 (Wendy Ann) ....each 400.00–500.00
   14–15" hp., 1947–1956, plus "Marme" (Margaret & Maggie) ....each 425.00 set 1,500.00
   14–15" hp., BK, plus "Marme" (Margaret & Maggie) ....each 375.00 set 1,500.00
   14–15" "Amy" with loop curls (Margaret) 475.00
   7½–8" hp., SLW, 1955, plus "Marme" (Wendy Ann) ....each 285.00 set 1,500.00
   8" hp., BKW, 1956–1959 (Wendy Ann) ....each 200.00 set 1,200.00
   8" BK, 1960–1972, (Wendy Ann) ....each 135.00 set 700.00
   8" straight leg, 1973–1975, marked "Alex." (Wendy Ann) ....each 60.00 set 350.00
   8" straight leg, 1976–1992 marked "Alexander" (Wendy Ann) (1985–1987 white face)...each 50.00–56.00
   11½–12" hp., jointed elbows & knees, 1957–1958 (Lissy) ....each 300.00 set 1,500.00

11½–12" hp., one-piece arms & legs, 1959–1966 (Lissy) ....each 225.00   set 1,100.00
12" plastic/vinyl, 1969–1982 (Nancy Drew) ....each 60.00   set 325.00
12" plastic/vinyl, 1983–1989, new outfits (Nancy Drew) ....each 60.00   set 325.00
12" set for Sears, 1989–1990 only (see Special Events/Exclusives)
LITTLEST KITTEN 8" vinyl, 1963, nude, clean, good face color 145.00
   Dressy, lacy oufit with bonnet 225.00
   Christening outfit 265.00
   Sewing or gift set ....800.00 up
   Play attire 150.00
LIVELY KITTEN 14", 18", 24", 1962–1963, knob makes limbs and head move 100.00–145.00
LIVELY HUGGUMS 25", 1963 only, knob makes limbs and head move.......................................100.00
LIVELY PUSSY CAT 14", 20", 24", 1966–1969, knob makes limbs and head move 100.00–150.00
LOLA AND LOLLIE BRIDESMAID 7" compo., 1938–1940 (Tiny Betty) ....each 285.00
LOLLIE BABY Rubber/compo, 1941–1942 ....95.00
LOOBY LOO 15½" hp., ca 1951–1954 ....800.00
LORD FAUNTLEROY 12", 1981–1983, Portrait Children (Nancy Drew)......................................70.00
LOUISA (see "Sound of Music")
LOVEY DOVE 19" vinyl baby, closed mouth, molded or rooted hair, 1958–1959..............................165.00
   19" hp./latex, 1950–1951 ....50.00–75.00
   12" all hp toddler, 1948–1951 (Precious)..350.00
LUCINDA 12" plastic/vinyl, 1969–1970 (Janie) 345.00
   14" plastic/vinyl, 1971–1982, blue gown (Mary Ann) 90.00
   14", 1983–1986, Classic Series, pink or peach gown (Mary Ann) 75.00
LUCK OF THE IRISH 8", 1992, Americana Series (Maggie Mixup) 55.00

8" LITTLEST KITTEN, 1963

15" hard plastic LITTLE WOMEN, 1950's

Lucy 8" hp., 1961 only, Americana Series (Wendy Ann) .... 2,100.00 up
Lucy Bride 14" hp., 1949–1950 (Margaret) 425.00
    17" hp., 1949–1950 (Margaret) 550.00
    16½" hp./vinyl arms, 1958 only (Elise) 350.00
    14" compo., 1937–1940 (Wendy Ann) 375.00
    17" compo., 1937–1940 (Wendy Ann) 475.00
    21" compo., 1942–1944 (Wendy Ann) 1,800.00
Lucy Locket 8" straight leg, 1986–1988, Storybook Series 75.00

7" Lollie Bridesmaid, 1938–1940

Please read "About Pricing" for additional information.

M.A.D.C. (MADAME ALEXANDER DOLL CLUB) (see Special Events/Exclusives)
MADAME BUTTERFLY 10", 1990, Marshall Fields (see Special Events/Exclusives)
MADAME DOLL 21" hp./vinyl arms, 1966 only, pink brocade (Coco) ....2,600.00 up
    14" plastic/vinyl, 1967–1975, Classic Series (Mary Ann) 375.00
MADAME (ALEXANDER) 21", 1984 only, one-piece skirt in pink 400.00
    21", 1985–1987, pink with overskirt that unsnaps 375.00
    21", 1988–1990, blue with full lace overskirt 345.00
MADAME POMPADOUR #2197, 21" hp./vinyl arms, 1970, pink lace overskirt (Jacqueline) 1,200.00
MADELAINE 14" compo., 1940–1942 (Wendy Ann)..550.00
    17–18" hp., 1949–1953 ....875.00
    8" hp., 1954, FAO Schwarz special 750.00
MADELAINE DU BAIN 11" compo., closed mouth, 1937 (Wendy Ann)...450.00
    14" compo., 1938–1939 (Wendy Ann) 575.00
    17" compo., 1939–1941 (Wendy Ann) 700.00
    21" compo., 1939–1941 (Wendy Ann) 825.00
    14" hp., 1949–1951 (Maggie) 950.00

14" MADELAINE DU BAIN, 1937

MADELINE 17–18" hp./jointed elbows & knees, 1950–1953 ....750.00
    18" hp., vinyl head, extra jointed body, 1961 only 785.00
    16½" Kelly, 1964 (Mary Ann) 450.00
    In trunk/wardrobe, various years ....700.00 up
MADISON, DOLLY 1976–1978, 1st set Presidents' Ladies/First Ladies Series (Martha) 120.00
MAGGIE 15" hp., 1948–1954 (Little Women only to 1956) 475.00
    17–18", 1949–1953 ....650.00
    20–21", 1948–1954 ....700.00
    22–23", 1949–1952 ....775.00
    17" plastic/vinyl, 1972–1973 only (Elise) 300.00
MAGGIE MIXUP 16½" hp./vinyl, 1960 only (Elise body) 350.00
    17" plastic/vinyl, 1961 only 225.00
    8" hp., 1960–1961 ....425.00
    8" hp. Angel, 1961 ....975.00
    8" in overalls/watering can, 1960–1961 ....650.00
    8" in skater outfit, 1960–1961 ....550.00
    8" in riding habit, 1960–1961 ....550.00
MAGGIE TEENAGER 15–18" hp., 1951–1953 ....500.00
    23", 1951–1953 ....685.00
MAGGIE WALKER 15–18" hp., 1949–1953 ....500.00
    20–21", 1949–1953 ....685.00
    23–25", 1951–1953 (With Cissy face) 650.00
MAGNOLIA #2297, 21", 1977 only, multi-rows lace on pink gown.................................400.00
    #2251, 21", 1988 only, yellow gown 275.00

18" MAGGIE, 1952

Maid Marian 8" hp., 1989–1991 only, Storybook Series (Wendy Ann)..60.00
 21", Portrait Series (Jacqueline) 305.00
Maid of Honor 18" compo., 1940–1944 (Wendy Ann)..700.00
 14" plastic/vinyl, 1988–1989, Classic Series (Mary Ann)...85.00
Majorette 14–17" compo., 1937–1938 (Wendy Ann)..850.00 up
 8" hp., 1955 only (Wendy Ann) 950.00
 8", 1991–1992, Americana Series, no baton 55.00
Mama Kitten #402, 18", 1963 only, knob moves head & limbs, cryer box......................................100.00
Mammy 8", 1989 only, Jubilee II set (black "round" face) 90.00
 8" hp., 1991–1992, Scarlett Series (black Wendy Ann) 55.00
Manet #2225, 21", 1982–1983, light brown with dark brown pinstripes (Jacqueline).....................275.00
 14", 1986–1987, Fine Arts Series (Mary Ann) 75.00
Marcella Dolls 13–24" compo., dressed in 1930's fashions, 1936 only......................each 500.00–800.00
March Hare Cloth/felt, mid 1930's 700.00
Margaret Rose (see Princess)
Margot 10–11" hp., 1961 only, formals (Cissette) ....385.00 up
 Street dresses, bathing suit, 1961 only 300.00
Margot Ballerina 15–18", 1953–1955 (Margaret & Maggie) 575.00
 15–18" hp./vinyl arms, 1955 only (Cissy) 450.00

14" Marine, 1942–1945
(Wendy Ann)

MARIA (see Sound of Music)
MARIE ANTOINETTE #2248, 21", 1987–1988, multi–floral print with pink front insert (Jacqueline) 285.00
MARINE 14" compo., 1943–1944 (Wendy Ann) 750.00
MARIONETTES/TONY SARG Compo., 1934–1940 .... 265.00
    12" compo., Disney 325.00
MARM LIZA 21" compo., 1938, 1946 (Wendy Ann) 2,200.00
MARME (see Little Women)
MARSHALL FIELDS (see Special Events/Exclusives)
MARTA (see Sound of Music)
MARTIN, MARY 14–17" hp., 1948–1952 (Margaret) 650.00–950.00
    14–17", in sailor suit, 1948–1952 .... 850.00–1,000.00
MARY ANN 14" plastic/vinyl, 1965 to date, still marked "1965" 75.00
    14" ballerina, 1973–1982 .... 150.00
MARYBEL (The doll that gets well) 16" rigid vinyl, 1959–1965 .... 200.00
    In case, 1959, 1961, 1965 .... 350.00
    In case with wardrobe, 1960 only 375.00
    In case/very long, straight hair, 1965 only 400.00
MARY CASSATT BABY 14" cloth/vinyl, 1969–1970 .... 150.00
    20", 1969–1970 .... 225.00
    14" plastic/vinyl child, 1987 only, Fine Arts Series (Mary Ann) 75.00
MARY ELLEN 31" rigid vinyl, walker, 1954 only 600.00
    31" plastic/vinyl arms, jointed elbows, non-walker, 1955 only 450.00

18" MARY MARTIN dolls, both original

15" MARY SUNSHINE, 1961 only

MARY ELLEN PLAYMATE 14" plastic/vinyl, 1965 only, Marshall Fields exclusive (Mary Ann) 300.00
    12" in case with wigs, 1965 (Lissy) 675.00
    17", 1965, exclusive 325.00
MARY GRAY 14" plastic/vinyl, 1988 only, Classic Series (Mary Ann) 75.00
MARY LOUISE 21" compo., 1938, 1946–1947 (Wendy Ann) 2,300.00
    18" hp., 1954 only, burnt orange & olive green, Me & My Shadow Series (Cissy) 1,400.00
    8" hp., 1954 only, same as 18" Me & My Shadow Series (Wendy Ann) 1,200.00
MARY, MARY 8" hp., BKW, 1965–1972, Storybook Series (Wendy Ann) 225.00
    8" hp., BK, 1965–1972 (Wendy Ann) 135.00
    8" hp., straight leg, 1973–1975, marked "Alex" 60.00
    8" hp., straight leg, 1976–1987, marked "Alexander" (1985–1987 white face) 55.00
    8", reintroduced 1992 (Wendy Ann) 55.00
    14", 1988–1991, Classic Series (Mary Ann) 75.00
MARY MINE 21" cloth/vinyl, 1977–1989 .... 125.00
    14" cloth/vinyl, 1977–1979 .... 75.00
    14", reintroduced 1989 .... 60.00
MARY MUSLIN 19" cloth, 1951 only, pansy eyes 400.00
    26", 1951 only 465.00
    40", 1951 only 600.00
MARY, QUEEN OF SCOTS #2252, 21", 1988–1989 (Jacqueline) 350.00
MARY ROSE BRIDE 17" hp., 1951 only (Margaret) 575.00
    16½", 1953, floral wreath circles near hem (Elise) 425.00
    10", 1957, floral wreath (Cissette) 375.00
MARY SUNSHINE 15" plastic/vinyl, 1961 (Caroline) 365.00
MCELROY, MARY 1985–1987, 4th set Presidents' Ladies/First Ladies Series (Mary Ann) 90.00
MCGUFFEY ANA 16" cloth, 1934–1936 .... 650.00
    7" compo., 1935–1939 (Tiny Betty) 300.00
    9" compo., 1935–1939 (Little Betty) 350.00

Beautiful, unplayed with, MCGUFFEY ANA, 1937

15" compo., 1935–1937 (Betty) 600.00
13" compo., 1938 (Wendy Ann) 675.00
11" closed mouth, 1937–1939 ....600.00
11–13" compo., 1937–1944 (Princess Elizabeth) 500.00–600.00
14–16" compo., 1937–1944 (Princess Elizabeth) 500.00–600.00
17–20" compo., 1937–1943 (Princess Elizabeth) 685.00–800.00
21–25" compo., 1937–1942 (Princess Elizabeth) 750.00–900.00
28" compo., 1937–1939 (Princess Elizabeth) 985.00
17" compo., 1948–1949 (Margaret) 775.00
14½" compo., 1948, coat, hat & muff 700.00
18", 25", 31", 1955–1956, flat feet (Cissy) 485.00–800.00
21" hp., 1948–1950 (Margaret) 850.00
12" hp., 1963 only (Lissy) ....1,200.00 up
8" hp., 1956 only (Wendy Ann) 625.00
8" hp., 1964–1965, was "American Girl" in 1962–1963 ....385.00
8", 1990–1991 only, Storybook Series (Wendy Ann) 55.00
29" cloth/vinyl, 1952 only (Barbara Jane) 485.00
14" plastic/vinyl, 1968–1969, plaid dress/eyelet apron, Classic Series (Mary Ann) 125.00
14" plastic/vinyl, 1977–1986, plaid dress, Classic Series (Mary Ann) 75.00
14" plastic/vinyl, 1987–1988, mauve stripe pinafore, Classic Series (Mary Ann) 70.00
McKee, Mary 1985–1987, 4th set Presidents' Ladies/First Ladies Series (Mary Ann) 90.00
McKinley, Ida 1988, 5th set Presidents' Ladies/First Ladies Series (Louisa) 85.00
Medici, Catherine de 21" porcelain, 1990–1991 ....525.00
Meg (see "Little Women")
Melanie 21" compo., 1945–1947 (Wendy Ann) 2,100.00
21" hp./vinyl arms, 1961, lace bodice & overdress over satin (Cissy) 750.00
#2050, 21", 1966, blue gown, wide lace down sides (Coco) 2,600.00
#2173, 1967, blue, white rick-rack around hem ruffle (Jacqueline) 575.00
#2181 1968, blue & white trim 550.00
#2193, 1969, blue gown, white trim, multi-rows of lace, bonnet 500.00
#2196, 1970, white gown, red ribbon trim 500.00
#2162, 1971, blue gown, white sequin trim 500.00
#2195, 1974, white gown, red jacket and bonnet 475.00
#2220, 1979, 1980 white dotted swiss gown with pink trim 350.00
1981, pink nylon with blue ribbon 300.00
#2254, 1989, all orange with lace shawl 300.00
10", 1969, pink multi-tiered skirt (Cissette) 425.00
10", 1970, yellow multi-tiered skirt 425.00
8" hp., 1955–1956 (Wendy Ann) 1,000.00
12", 1987 only, aqua green gown, brown trim, Portrait Children Series (Nancy Drew) 75.00
#1101, 10", 1989 only, all royal blue, black trim, Jubilee II (Cissette) 85.00
8", 1990, lavender/lace, Scarlett Series (Wendy Ann) 65.00
8", 1992, peach gown/bonnet with lace 57.00
Melinda 10" hp., 1968, blue gown with white trim (Cissette) 350.00
1970, yellow multi-tiered lace skirt 350.00
16–22" plastic/vinyl, 1962–1963 ....365.00
14", 16", 22" plastic/vinyl, 1963 ....250.00–425.00
14" ballerina, 1963 only 325.00
Melody and Friend 25" and 8" (see Special Events/Exclusives)
Merry Angel 8", 1991, Spiegels (see Special Events/Exclusives)
Metroplex Doll Club (see Special Events/Exclusives)
Mexico 7" compo., 1936 (Tiny Betty) 265.00
9" compo., 1938–1939 (Little Betty) 285.00

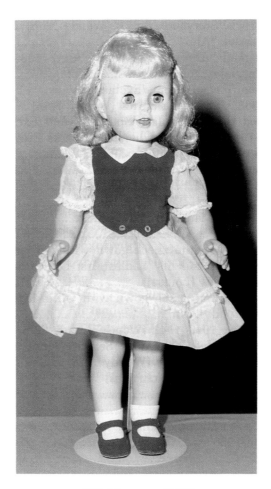

22" MELINDA, 1962

8" hp., BKW, 1964–1965 (Wendy Ann) 150.00
8" hp., BK, 1965–1972 ....135.00
8" straight leg, 1973–1975, marked "ALEX" 60.00
8" straight leg, 1976–1991, marked "Alexander" (1985–1987 white face) 55.00
1985, white face 60.00
MICHAEL 11" plastic/vinyl, 1969 only (Janie) 300.00
 With teddy bear, mint condition 450.00
 8", 1992, Storybook Series (Wendy Ann) 52.00
MIDNIGHT #2256, 21", 1990, dark blue/black (Jacqueline) 250.00
MILLY 17" plastic/vinyl, 1968 only (Polly) 500.00
MIMI 30", multi-jointed body, (hp. in 1961 only), in formal 800.00
 Romper suit/skirt 550.00
 Tyrolean outfit 900.00
 Slacks, stripe top, straw hat 550.00
 Red sweater, plaid skirt 550.00
 #2170, 21" hp./vinyl arms, 1971, vivid pink cape & trim on white gown (Jacqueline) 525.00
 14", 1983–1986, Opera Series (Mary Ann) 90.00
MISS AMERICA 14" compo., 1941–1943, holds flag 750.00
MISS LEIGH 8", 1989, for C.U. Gathering (see Special Events/Exclusives)
MISS LIBERTY 10", M.A.D.C. (see Special Events/Exclusives)
MISS MAGNIN 1991, I. Magnin (see Special Events/Exclusives)

O

Please read "About Pricing" for additional information.

O'BRIEN, MARGARET 14½" compo., 1946–1948 ....700.00
    17", 18", 19" compo., 1946–1948 ....850.00–975.00
    21–24" compo., 1946–1948 ....950.00–1,200.00
    14½" hp., 1949–1951 ....875.00
    17–18" hp., 1949–1951 ....1,000.00
    21–22" hp., 1949–1951 ....1,250.00
OLD FASHIONED GIRL 13" compo., 1945–1947 (Betty) 425.00
    20" hp., 1948 only (Margaret)...700.00
    14" hp., 1948 only (Margaret)...650.00
OLIVER TWIST 16" cloth, 1934, Dicken's character 625.00
    7" compo., 1935–1936 (Tiny Betty) 285.00
    8", 1992, Storyland Series (Wendy Ann) 50.00
OLIVER TWISTAIL Cloth/felt, 1930's 700.00
OPENING NIGHT 10", 1989 only, Portrette (Cissette)..75.00
OPHELIA 12", 1992, Romance Collection (Nancy Drew) 115.00
ORCHARD PRINCESS 21" compo., 1939, 1946–1947 (Wendy Ann) 2,200.00
ORPHANT ANNIE 14" plastic/vinyl, 1965–1966 only, Literature Series (Mary Ann)...........425.00

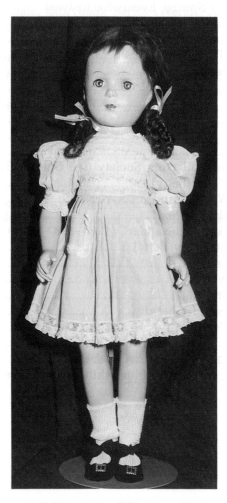

21" MARGARET O'BRIEN, 1949

P

Please read "About Pricing" for additional information.

PAMELA 12" hp., 1962–1963 only, takes wigs (Lissy) 475.00
   In case or window box, 1962–1963 ....1,200.00
   12" plastic/vinyl, 1969–1971 (Nancy Drew) 250.00
   In case, 1969 ....450.00 up
PAN AMERICAN–POLLERA 7" compo., 1936–1938 (Tiny Betty) 300.00
PANAMA 8", 1985–1987 ....90.00
PANDORA 8", 1991, Dolls 'n Bearland (see Special Events/Exclusives)
PARLOUR MAID 8" hp., 1956 only (Wendy Ann) 1,600.00
PATCHITY PAM & PEPPER 15" cloth, 1965–1966 ....125.00
PATTERSON, MARTHA JOHNSON 1982–1984, 3rd set Presidents' Ladies/First Ladies Series (Martha) 95.00
PATTY 18" plastic/vinyl, 1965 only 225.00
PATTY PIGTAILS 14" hp., 1949 only (Margaret) 800.00
PAULETTE 10", 1989, 1990 only, Portrette (Cissette) 90.00
PEARL (JUNE) 10", 1992, Birthstone Collection 64.00
PEASANT 7" compo., 1936–1937 (Tiny Betty) 265.00
   9" compo., 1938–1939 (Little Betty) 285.00
PEGGY BRIDE 14–18" hp., 1950–1951 (Margaret) 575.00
   21" hp., 1950 ....750.00

Wonderful, never played with, PAMELA, 1962
(Lissy)

···◄ P ►···

PENNY 34" cloth/vinyl, 1951 only 450.00
  42", 1951 only 600.00
  7" compo., 1938–1940 (Tiny Betty) 285.00
PERSIA 7" compo., 1936–1938 (Tiny Betty) 300.00
PERU 8", 1986–1987 ....90.00
PERUVIAN BOY 8" hp., BK, 1965–1966 (Wendy Ann)...400.00
  8" hp., BKW 475.00
PETER PAN 15" hp., 1953–1954 (Margaret) 800.00
  8" hp., 1953–1954 (Wendy Ann)..1,200.00
  8" hp., reintroduced, 1991–1992, Storyland Series (Wendy Ann) 52.00
  14" plastic/vinyl, 1969 only (Mary Ann) 385.00
  Complete set of 4 dolls, 1969 only (Peter, Michael, Wendy, Tinkerbelle) 1,400.00
PHILIPPINES 8" straight leg, 1986–1987 ....75.00
  1987, in yellow gown 95.00
PICNIC DAY 18" hp., 1953 only, Glamour Girl Series (Margaret) 1,250.00
PIERCE, JANE 1982–1984, 3rd set Presidents' Ladies/First Ladies Series (Mary Ann) 95.00
PIERROT CLOWN 8" hp., 1956 only (Wendy Ann) 1,350.00
  14", 1991–1992, Classic Series (Mary Ann) 80.00
PILGRIM 7" compo., 1935–1938 (Tiny Betty) 275.00
PINKY 16" cloth, 1940's 475.00
  23" compo./cloth baby, 1937–1939 ....165.00
  13–19" vinyl baby, 1954 only 65.00–95.00
  12" plastic/vinyl, 1975–1987, Portrait Children Series (Nancy Drew) 65.00
PINOCCHIO 8", 1992, Storyland Series (Wendy Ann)...55.00
PIP All cloth, early 1930's, Dickens character 800.00
  7" compo., 1935–1936 (Tiny Betty) 285.00
PITTY PAT 16" cloth, 1950's 400.00
PITTY PAT CLOWN 1950's 450.00
PLAYMATES 29" cloth, 1940's 250.00–450.00
POCAHONTAS 8" hp., BK, 1967–1970, Americana & Storyland Series (Wendy Ann) 475.00
  8" hp., reintroduced 1991, Americana Series (Wendy Ann) 52.00
POLISH (POLAND) 8" hp., BKW, 1964–1965 (Wendy Ann)...200.00
  8" BKW, 1965 only (Maggie Mixup) 250.00
  8" hp., BK, 1965–1972 ....135.00
  8" hp., straight leg, 1973–1975, marked "ALEX." 60.00
  8" straight leg, 1976–1988, marked "Alexander" (1985–1987 white face)...................55.00
  7" compo., 1935–1936 (Tiny Betty) 265.00
  8", reintroduced 1992 (Maggie Mixup) 65.00
POLK, SARAH 1979–1981, 2nd set Presidents' Ladies/First Ladies Series (Martha) 105.00
POLLERA (PAN AMERICAN) 7" compo., 1936–1937 (Tiny Betty)................................285.00
POLLY 17" plastic/vinyl, 1965 only...325.00
  Ballgown 400.00
  Street dress 325.00
  Ballerina 300.00
  Bride 325.00
  In Trunk/Wardrobe, 1965 only 800.00
POLLY FLINDERS 8", 1988–1989, Storybook Series (Maggie) 90.00
POLLY PIGTAILS 14½" hp., 1949–1951 (Maggie) 650.00
  17–17½", 1949–1951 ....875.00
  8" hp., 1990, M.A.D.C. (see Special Events/Exclusives)
POLLY PUT KETTLE ON 7" compo., 1937–1939 (Tiny Betty) 265.00
POLLYANA 16" rigid vinyl, 1960–1961, marked "1958" (Marybel) 400.00
  In formal 500.00

22", 1960–1961 ....450.00
14", 1987–1988, Classic Series (Mary Ann) 75.00
8", 1992, Storyland Series (Maggie Mixup) 65.00
POODLES 14–17", 1940's, standing or sitting 250.00
POOR CINDERELLA (see Cinderella)
POPPY 9" early vinyl, 1953 only, orange organdy dress & bonnet 95.00
PORTRAIT ELISE 17" plastic/vinyl, 1972–1973 ....200.00
PORTUGAL 8" hp., BK, 1968–1972 (Wendy Ann)...135.00
8" straight leg, 1973–1975, marked "Alex." 60.00
8" straight leg, 1976–1987, marked "Alexander" 55.00
8", 1986, white face 55.00
POSEY PET 15" cloth, 1940's, plush rabbit or other animals 500.00
PRECIOUS 12" compo./cloth baby, 1937–1940 ....145.00
12" all hp. toddler, 1948–1951 ....350.00

12" PRECIOUS, 1948–1951
(Also LOVEY DOVEY)

PREMIER DOLLS 8", 1990–1991 (see Special Events/Exclusives)
PRESIDENTS' LADIES/FIRST LADIES
1st set, 1976–1978	120.00 singles	850.00 set
2nd set, 1979–1981	105.00 singles	625.00 set
3rd set, 1982–1984	95.00 singles	575.00 set
4th set, 1985–1987	90.00 singles	550.00 set
5th set, 1988	85.00 singles	475.00 set
6th set, 1989–1990	100.00 singles	600.00 set

PRINCE CHARLES 8" hp., 1957 only (Wendy Ann) 650.00
PRINCE CHARMING 16–17" compo., 1947 (Margaret) 650.00
   14–15" hp., 1948–1950 (Margaret) 775.00
   17–18" hp., 1948–1950 (Margaret) 875.00
   21" hp., 1949–1951 (Margaret) 975.00
   12", 1990–1991, Romance Collection (Nancy Drew) 90.00
PRINCE PHILLIP 17–18" hp., 1953 only, Beaux Arts Series (Margaret) 750.00
   21", 1953 only 850.00
PRINCESS 12", 1990–1992, Romance Collection (Nancy Drew) 92.00
   14", 1990 (Mary Ann) (1991 Jennifer) 140.00
   20" hp., 1955 only, Child's Dream Comes True Series (Cissy) 800.00
PRINCESS ALEXANDRIA 24" cloth/compo., 1937 only ....225.00 up
PRINCESS ANN 8" hp., 1957 only (Wendy Ann) 800.00
PRINCESS DOLL 13–15" compo., 1940–1942 (Princess Elizabeth) 525.00
   24" compo., 1940–1942 (Princess Elizabeth) 775.00
PRINCESS ELIZABETH 7" compo., 1937–1939 (Tiny Betty) 300.00
   8" with Dionne head, 1937 ....250.00
   9–11" compo., 1937–1941 (Little Betty) 350.00–400.00
   13" compo with closed mouth, 1937–1941 ....500.00
   14" compo., 1937–1941 ....500.00
   15" compo., open mouth 525.00
   18–19" compo., open mouth, 1937–1941 ....625.00
   24" compo., open mouth, 1938–1939 ....750.00
   28" compo., open mouth, 1938–1939 ....950.00
PRINCESS FLAVIA (ALSO VICTORIA) 21" compo., 1939, 1946–1947 (Wendy Ann) ...2,300.00
PRINCESS MARGARET ROSE 15–18" compo., 1937–1938 (Princess Elizabeth) ...775.00
   21" compo., 1938 ....965.00
   14–18" hp., 1949–1953 (Margaret) 775.00
   18" hp., 1953 only, Beaux Art Series, pink taffeta gown & tiara (Margaret) ...1,300.00
PRINCESS ROSETTA 21" compo., 1939, 1946–1947 (Wendy Ann) 2,000.00
PRISCILLA 18" cloth, mid 1930's 650.00
   7" compo., 1935–1938 (Tiny Betty) 285.00
   8" hp., BK, 1965–1970, Americana & Storybook Series (Wendy Ann) ...375.00
PRISSY 8", 1990 only, Scarlett Series (Wendy Ann) 57.00
   8", reintroduced 1992 ....50.00
PROM QUEEN (see M.A.D.C. under Special Events/Exclusives)
PUDDIN' 14–21" cloth/vinyl, 1966–1975 ....85.00
   14–18", 1987 ....75.00
   14–21", 1990–1992 ....95.00–105.00
PUMPKIN 22" cloth/vinyl, 1967–1976 ....145.00
   22" with rooted hair, 1976 only 165.00
PUSSY CAT 14–18" cloth/vinyl, 1965–1992 ....95.00
   Lively, 14", 20", 24", 1966–1969, knob makes head & limbs move 95.00
   14" black, 1974–1979 ....95.00
   14" black, reintroduced 1991–1992 ....85.00–105.00
   14", 1966, 1968, in trunk/trousseau ....350.00 up
   20" white or black 100.00
   24" 125.00

Please read "About Pricing" for additional information.

QUEEN 18" hp., 1953 only, white gown, velvet long cape trimmed with fur,
Beaux Arts Series (Margaret) 1,400.00
 18" hp., 1953 only (same gown/tiara as above but no cape), Glamour Girl Series (Margaret).... 950.00
 18" hp., 1954 only, white gown, short orlon cape, Me & My Shadow Series (Margaret) 1,350.00
 8" hp., 1954, orlon cape attached to purple robe,
Me & My Shadow Series (Wendy Ann) 1,400.00
 8" scarlet velvet robe, 1955 only 950.00
 10" hp., 1957–1959, gold gown, blue ribbon (Cissette) 425.00
 1960–1963, white gown, blue ribbon 450.00
 10" hp., 1972, 1973, 1974, white gown, red ribbon (Cissette) 350.00
 In trunk/wardrobe, 1959 (Cissette) .... 900.00 up
 14", 1990 only, Classic Series (Louisa, Jennifer) 90.00
 20" hp./vinyl arms, 1955, white brocade, Dream Come True Series (Cissy) 850.00
 1957, white gown, Fashion Parade Series 850.00
 1958, 1961–1963, gold gown (1958, Dolls To Remember Series) 800.00

QUEEN, 1965

18" Elise, 1963 only, white gown, red ribbon 750.00
    With Marybel head 775.00
18" vinyl with Elise head, gold brocade gown (same as 1965)
    (21", rooted hair, 1966 only), rare 1,200.00
#2150, 21" hp./vinyl arms, 1965, gold brocade gown (Jacqueline) 750.00
    1968, gold gown 700.00
QUEEN ALEXANDRINE 21" compo., 1939–1941 (Wendy Ann) 2,000.00
QUEEN CHARLOTTE 10", 1991, M.A.D.C. (see Special Events/Exclusives)
QUEEN ELIZABETH I 10", 1990, My Doll House (see Special Events/Exclusives)
QUEEN ELIZABETH II 8", 1992, 40th anniversary (1953), mid-year introduction (limited to 1992) 130.00
QUEEN OF HEARTS 8" straight leg, 1987–1990, Storybook Series (Wendy Ann) 90.00
    8", Disney, 1992, #3 Annual Showcase of Dolls (see Special Events/Exclusives)
QUINTUPLETS (FISHER QUINTS) Hp., 1964, (Genius) ....set 600.00
QUIZ-KINS 8" hp., 1953, in romper only (Wendy Ann) 475.00
    Groom, 1953–1954 ....600.00
    Girl with wig, 1953–1954 ....675.00
    Girl without wig, in romper suit 425.00
    Bride, 1953–1954 ....550.00

18" QUEEN using Elise doll, 1963

Please read "About Pricing" for additional information.

RACHEL (some tagged Rachael) 8", 1989, Belk's (see Special Events/Exclusives)
RANDOLPH, MARTHA 1976–1978, 1st set First Ladies/Presidents' Ladies Series (Louisa) 120.00
RAPUNZEL 10", 1989–1992, Portrette (Cissette) 115.00
REBECCA 14–17", 21" compo., 1940–1941 (Wendy Ann) 600.00–1,400.00
 14" hp., 1948–1949 (Margaret)...900.00
 14" plastic/vinyl, Classic Series, 1968–1969, two-tiered skirt in pink (Mary Ann)......................250.00
  1970–1985, one-piece skirt, pink pindot or check dress 75.00
  1986–1987, blue dress with striped pinafore...60.00

14" REBECCA, 1986–1987

RED BOY 8" hp., BK, 1972 (Wendy Ann)...135.00
 1973–1975, marked "Alex." 60.00
 1976–1988, marked "Alexander" (1985–1987 white face) 55.00
RED CROSS NURSE 7" compo., 1937, 1941–1943 (Tiny Betty) 285.00
 9" compo., 1939, 1942–1943 (Little Betty)...300.00
 14" hp., 1948 only (Margaret)...875.00
RED RIDING HOOD 7" compo., 1936–1942 (Tiny Betty) 285.00
 9" compo., 1939–1940 (Little Betty) 300.00
 8" hp., SLW, 1955 (Wendy Ann)...450.00
 8" hp., BKW, 1962–1965, Storybook Series (Wendy Ann) 325.00
 8" hp., BK, 1965–1972 ....135.00
 8" hp., straight leg, 1973–1975, marked "Alex." 60.00
 8" hp., straight leg, 1976–1986, marked "Alexander" (1985–1987 white face) 55.00
 8", 1987–1991 (Maggie), 1992 (Wendy Ann) 55.00

RENOIR 21" compo., 1945–1946 (Wendy Ann) 2,200.00
   14" hp., 1950 only (Margaret) 875.00
   21" hp./vinyl arms, 1961 only (Cissy)..850.00
   18" hp./vinyl arms, vinyl head, 1963 only (Elise) 600.00
   #2154, 21" hp./vinyl arms, 1965, pink gown (Jacqueline)................................700.00
      #2062, 1966, blue gown with black trim (Coco) 2,300.00
      #2175, 1967, navy blue gown, red hat 650.00
      #2194, #2184, 1969–1970, blue gown, full lace overdress........................650.00
      #2163, 1971, all yellow gown 650.00
      #2190, 1972, pink gown with black jacket & trim 650.00
      #2190, 1973, yellow gold gown, black ribbon..625.00
   10" hp., 1968, all navy with red hat (Cissette) 450.00
      1969, pale blue gown, short jacket, stripe or dotted skirt.........................500.00
      1970, all aqua satin 425.00
RENOIR CHILD 12" plastic/vinyl, 1967 only, Portrait Children Series (Nancy Drew)............165.00
   14", 1968 only (Mary Ann) 200.00
RENOIR GIRL 14" plastic/vinyl, 1967–1968, white dress, red ribbon trim,
Portrait Children Series (Mary Ann)..200.00
   1969–1971, pink dress, white pinafore 90.00
   1972–1986, pink multi–tiered lace gown 70.00
   1986 only, pink pleated nylon dress 70.00

21" RENOIR PORTRAIT, 1969–1970

RENOIR GIRL WITH WATERING CAN 1986–1987, Classics & Fine Arts Series 75.00
    With hoop, 1986–1987, Classic & Fine Arts Series 75.00
RENOIR MOTHER 21" hp./vinyl arms, 1967 only, navy blue, red hat (Jacqueline) 900.00
RHETT 12", 1981–1985, Portrait Children Series (Nancy Drew)..85.00
    #401, 8" Jubilee II, 1989 only (Wendy Ann)..95.00
    8", 1991–1992, Scarlett Series...57.00
RIDING HABIT 8", 1990 only, Americana Series (Wendy Ann) 90.00
RIDING HOOD 16" cloth/felt, 1930's 650.00
RILEY'S LITTLE ANNIE 14" plastic/vinyl, 1967 only, Literature Series (Mary Ann) 175.00
RINGBEARER 14" hp., 1951 only (Lovey Dove) 500.00
RINGMASTER 8", C.U. (see Special Events/Exclusives)
RIVERBOAT QUEEN (LENA) M.A.D.C. (see Special Events/Exclusives)
ROBIN HOOD 8", 1988–1990, Storybook Series (Wendy Ann)..85.00
RODEO 8" hp., 1955 only (Wendy Ann) 900.00
ROGERS, GINGER 14–21" compo., 1940–1945 (Wendy Ann) ....1,200.00 up
ROLLER SKATING 8" hp., 1953–1955 (Wendy Ann) 500.00
ROMANCE 21" compo., 1945–1946 (Wendy Ann)...2,000.00
ROMEO 18" compo., 1949 (Wendy Ann) 1,400.00
    8" hp., 1955 only (Wendy Ann) 1,300.00
    12" plastic/vinyl, 1978–1987, Portrait Children Series (Nancy Drew) 75.00
    12" reintroduced, 1991–1992, Romance Series (Nancy Drew) 92.00

14" RENOIR WITH HOOP, 1986–1987

R

ROOSEVELT, EDITH   1988, 5th set Presidents' Ladies/First Ladies Series (Louisa) 85.00
ROOSEVELT, ELEANOR   14", 1989–1990, 6th set Presidents' Ladies/First Ladies Series (Louisa) 100.00
ROSAMUND BRIDESMAID   15" hp., 1951 only (Margaret) 685.00
    18" hp., 1951 only 700.00
ROSE   9" early vinyl toddler, 1953 only, pink organdy dress & bonnet 100.00
ROSEBUD   16–19" cloth/vinyl, 1952–1953 ....135.00
    13", 1953 only 160.00
    23–25", 1953 only 185.00
ROSEBUD (PUDDIN')   14"–20", 1986 only, white 60.00
    14", black 65.00
ROSE FAIRY   8" hp., 1956 only (Wendy Ann) ....1,800.00 up
ROSETTE   10", 1987–1989, Portrette Series (Cissette) 75.00
ROSEY POSEY   14" cloth/vinyl, 1976 only 65.00
    21" cloth/vinyl, 1976 only 95.00
ROSS, BETSY   8" hp., Americana Series, 1967–1972 (Wendy Ann)
    Bend knees 135.00
    Straight legs, Storybook Series, 1973–1975, marked "Alex" 60.00
    Straight legs, 1976–1987, (1985–1987 white face) 55.00
    8" reintroduced, 1991–1992, Americana Series 55.00
    1976 Bicentennial gown (stars) 125.00
ROSY   14", 1988–1990 (Mary Ann) 75.00
ROYAL EVENING   18" hp., 1953 only (Margaret) 1,400.00
ROYAL WEDDING   21" compo., 1939 only (Wendy Ann) 2,300.00
ROZY   12" plastic/vinyl, 1969 only (Janie) 450.00
RUBY (JULY)   10", 1992, Birthstone Collection (Cissette) 64.00
RUFFLES CLOWN   21", 1954 only 400.00
RUMBERA/RUMBERO   7" compo., 1938–1943 (Tiny Betty) ....each 235.00
    9" compo., 1939–1941 (Little Betty) ....each 300.00
RUMANIA   8" hp., BK, 1968–1972 (Wendy Ann) 135.00
    8" straight leg, 1973–1975, marked "Alex." 60.00
    8" straight leg, 1976–1987, marked "Alexander" 55.00
    8", 1986, white face 55.00
RUMPELSTILTSKIN & MILLER'S DAUGHTER   8" & 14", 1992, limited to 3,000 sets 232.00
RUSSIA   8" hp., BK, 1968–1972 (Wendy Ann) 135.00
    8" straight leg, 1973–1975, marked "Alex." 60.00
    8" straight leg, 1976–1988, marked "Alexander" (1985–1987 white face) 55.00
    8", 1985–1987, white face 55.00
    8", reintroduced 1991–1992 ....52.00
RUSSIAN   7" compo., 1935–1938 (Tiny Betty) 265.00
RUSTY   20" cloth/vinyl, 1967–1968 only 350.00

Please read "About Pricing" for additional information.

SAILOR 14" compo., 1942–1945 (Wendy Ann) 750.00
  17" compo., 1943–1944 ....900.00
  8" boy, 1990, U.F.D.C. (see Special Events/Exclusives)
  8" boy, 1991, FAO Schwarz (see Special Events/Exclusives)
SAILORETTE 10" hp., 1988 only, Portrette Series (Cissette) 75.00
SALLY BRIDE 14" compo., 1938–1939 (Wendy Ann) 425.00
  18–21" compo., 1938–1939 ....485.00
SALOME 14", 1984–1986, Opera Series (Mary Ann) 90.00
SAMANTHA 1989, FAO Schwarz (see Special Events/Exclusives)
  14", 1991–1992, Classic Series, gold ruffled gown (Mary Ann) 170.00
SANDY McHARE Cloth/felt, 1930's 650.00
SAPPHIRE (SEPTEMBER) 10", 1992, Birthstone Collection 64.00
SARDINIA 8", 1989–1991 only (Wendy Ann) 55.00
SARGENT 14", 1984–1985, dressed in lavender, Fine Arts Series (Mary Ann) 75.00
SARGENT'S GIRL 14", 1986 only, dressed in pink, Fine Arts Series (Mary Ann) 75.00
SCARLETT O'HARA (pre-movie, 1937–1938)
  7" compo., 1937–1942 (Tiny Betty) 365.00
  9" compo., 1938–1941 (Little Betty) 425.00
  11", 1937–1942 (Wendy Ann) 550.00
  14–15" compo., 1941–1943 (Wendy Ann) 600.00

SCARLETT (Also SOUTHERN GIRL)
1942–1943

18" compo., 1939–1946 (Wendy Ann) 1,000.00
21" compo., 1945, 1947 (Wendy Ann) 1,400.00
14–16" hp., 1950's (Margaret) 1,200.00
14–16" hp., 1950's (Maggie) 1,200.00
20" hp., 1950's (Margaret) ....1,300.00 up
18" hp./vinyl arms, 1963 only, pale blue organdy w/rosebuds, straw hat (Elise) 900.00
12" hp., 1963 only, green taffeta gown and bonnet (Lissy) 1,400.00
21", 1955, 1961–1962, blue taffeta gown w/black looped braid trim (Cissy) 1,300.00
7½–8", 1953–1954, white gown w/red rosebuds, white lace hat (Wendy Ann) 1,000.00
7½–8" hp., 1955, two layer gown, white/yellow/green trim (Wendy Ann)..................................950.00
8" hp., BKW, 1956, pink or blue floral gown 950.00
8" hp., BKW, 1957, white, lace and ribbon trim 950.00
8" BK, 1965, in white gown (Wendy Ann) 750.00
8" BK, 1966–1972, flowered gown, Americana & Storybook Series 425.00
8", 1973–1992, in white gown (Wendy Ann) 57.00
   Straight leg, marked "Alex." 65.00
   Straight leg, 1976–1986, marked "Alexander" (1985–1986 white face)..................60.00
   1987 white face, blue dot gown 225.00
   Straight leg, 1988–1989, flowered gown 60.00
   1986, M.A.D.C. (see Special Events/Exclusives)
   1989, Child At Heart (see Special Events/Exclusives)
   Straight leg, 1990 only, tiny floral print 60.00
   1991 only, 3-tier white gown, curly hair 65.00
   1992, rose floral print, oversized bonnet 65.00

21" SCARLETT, 1965

SCARLETT, 1968

SCARLETT, 1991

8" hp., 1990, M.A.D.C. Symposium (see Special Events/Exclusives)
21" hp./vinyl arms, 1965, #2152, green satin gown (Jacqueline) 1,200.00
    #2061, 1966, all white gown, red sash & roses (Also with plain wide lace hem;
        also inverted "V" scalloped lace hem – allow more for this gown.) (Coco) 2,700.00
    #2174, 1967, green satin gown with black trim..950.00
    #2180, 1968, floral print gown with wide white hem 1,000.00
    #2190, 1969, red gown with white lace...725.00
    #2180, 1970, green satin, white trim on jacket...800.00
    #2292, 2295, 2296, 1975–1977, all green satin, white lace at cuffs..750.00
    #2110, 1978, silk floral gown, green parasol, white lace 725.00
    #2240, 1979–1985, green velvet 325.00
    #2255, 1986 only, floral gown, green parasol, white lace 350.00
    #2247, 1987–1988, layered all over white gown...325.00
    #2253, 1989, doll has full bangs, all red gown 300.00
    #2258, 1990–1992, Bride, Scarlett Series 355.00
    #2259, 1991–1992, green on white, three ruffles around skirt 282.00
    #009, 1991 only, porcelain, green velvet, gold trim...585.00
10" hp., 1968 only, lace in bonnet, green satin gown with black braid trim (Cissette)..............475.00
    1969, green satin gown with white & gold braid 450.00
    1970–1973, green satin gown with gold braid trim..450.00
    1990–1991 only, Scarlett Series, floral print gown 85.00
10", 1992, Scarlett at Ball, all in black..90.00
12", 1981–1985, green gown with braid trim (Nancy Drew) 85.00
14" plastic/vinyl, 1968, floral gown (Mary Ann)...450.00
    1969–1986, white gown with five rows of lace (Mary Ann) 145.00
    1987–1989, blue floral print 145.00
    1990, Scarlett Series, tiny floral print gown..135.00
    1991–1992, Scarlett Series, white ruffles, green ribbon (Louisa) 147.00
Jubilee #1, #1500, 14", 1986 only, all green velvet (Mary Ann)...165.00
Jubilee #2, #1300, 14", 1989 only, green floral print gown (Mary Ann) 100.00
    #1100, 10", burgundy & white gown (Cissette) 100.00
    #400, 8", all green velvet gown (Wendy Ann) 145.00

SCARLETT, MISS 14", 1988, Belk's Department Store (see Special Events/Exclusives)
SCASSI GOWN 21", 1990, FAO Schwarz (see Special Events/Exclusives)
SCHOOL GIRL 7" compo., 1936–1943 (Tiny Betty) 285.00
SCOTCH 7" compo., 1936–1939 (Tiny Betty) 265.00
    9" compo., 1939–1940 (Little Betty) 285.00
    10" hp., 1962–1963 (Cissette)..1,200.00
SCOTS LASS 8" hp., BKW, 1963 only (Maggie Mixup, Wendy Ann)..............................250.00
SCOTTISH (SCOTLAND) 8" hp., BKW, 1964–1965 (Wendy Ann) 250.00
    8" hp., BK, 1965–1972 ....135.00
    8" straight leg, 1973–1975, marked "ALEX." 60.00
    8" straight leg, 1976–1992, marked "Alexander" (1985–1987 white face) 52.00
SCOUTING 8", 1991–1992, Americana Series 55.00
SEARS ROEBUCK (see Special Events/Exclusives)
SEPTEMBER 14", 1989 only, Classic Series (Mary Ann) 75.00
SEVEN DWARFS Compo., 1937 only..each 675.00
SHAHARAZAD 10", 1992, Portrette Series (Cissette)..84.00
SHEA ELF 8", 1990, C.U. (see Special Events/Exclusives)
SHIRLEY'S DOLL HOUSE (see Special Events/Exclusives)
SICILY 8", 1989–1990 (Wendy Ann) 75.00
SIMONE 21" hp./vinyl arms, 1968 only, in trunk (Jacqueline) ....1,600.00 up
SIR LAPIN HARE Cloth/felt, 1930's 650.00
SISTER BRENDA (see FAO Swartz under Special Events/Exclusives)
SITTING PRETTY 18" foam body, 1965 only...400.00
SKATER 8", 1991, C.U. (see Special Events/Exclusives)
SKATER'S WALTZ 15"–18", 1955–1956 (Cissy) 600.00
SKATING DOLL (Sonja Henie untagged) 16", 1944–1947 ....575.00
SLEEPING BEAUTY 7–9" compo., 1941–1944 (Tiny Betty & Little Betty) 300.00
    15–16" compo., 1938–1940 (Princess Elizabeth) 400.00
    18–21" compo., 1941–1944 (Wendy Ann) 550.00
    10" hp., 1960 (Cissette)...475.00
    10" Portrette Series, 1991–1992 ....95.00
    16½" hp., 1959 (Elise)..550.00
    21", 1959 only 875.00
    10" hp., 1959 only, in blue for Disneyland (Cissette) 465.00
    12", 1990, for Disney (see Special Events/Exclusives)
    14" plastic/vinyl, 1971–1985, Classic Series, gold gown (Mary Ann) 75.00
    14", 1986–1990, Classic Series, blue gown (Mary Ann)..90.00
SLUMBERMATE 12" cloth/compo., 1940's 465.00
    21" compo/cloth, 1940's 550.00
    13" vinyl/cloth, 1951 only 125.00
SMARTY 12" plastic/vinyl, 1962–1963..325.00
    Smarty & Baby, 1963 only 400.00
    With boy "Artie" in case with wardrobe, 1963 only...600.00
SMILEY 20" cloth/vinyl, 1971 only (Happy) 265.00
SMOKEY TAIL Cloth/felt, 1930's 650.00
SNOWFLAKE M.A.D.C. (see Special Events/Exclusives)
SNOW WHITE 13" compo., 1937–1939, painted eyes (Princess Elizabeth) 400.00
    12" compo., 1939–1940 (Princess Elizabeth)..400.00
    13" compo, 1939–1940, sleep eyes (Princess Elizabeth) 385.00
    16" compo., 1939–1942 (Princess Elizabeth)..475.00
    18" compo., 1939–1940 (Princess Elizabeth)..600.00
    14–15" hp., 1952 only (Margaret) 550.00–800.00
    18–23", 1952 only...800.00–1,000.00

21" hp. (Margaret) 1,100.00

14", 1967–1977, Disney Crest Color. (#1455) (Mary Ann)..475.00

8" hp., 1972–1977, Disney Crest Colors (Wendy Ann) 475.00

8", 1990–1992, Storyland Series (Wendy Ann)..55.00

12", 1990, Disney (see Special Events/Exclusives)

14" plastic/vinyl, 1968–1985, white gown, Classic Series (Mary Ann) 200.00

1986–1992, ecru & gold gown, red cape (Mary Ann, Louisa) 120.00

Snow Queen 10", 1991–1992, Portrette Series (Cissette)...84.00

So Big 22" cloth/vinyl, 1968–1975, painted eyes 250.00

So Lite Baby or Toddler 20" cloth, 1930's ....450.00 up

Soldier 14" compo., 1943–1944 (Wendy Ann) 750.00

17" compo., 1942–1945 (Wendy Ann) 850.00

Sound of Music, large set, 1965–1970

14" Louisa (Mary Ann) 300.00

10" Friedrich (Smarty) 200.00

14" Brigitta, 14" Liesl (Mary Ann) ....each 225.00

10" Marta, 10" Gretl (Smarty)..each 200.00

17" Maria (Elise or Polly) 375.00

Full set of 7 dolls 1,700.00

Sound of Music, small set, 1971–1973

12" Maria (Nancy Drew)...350.00

8" Marta, 8" Friedrich, 8" Gretl (Wendy Ann) ....each 225.00

10" Brigitta (Cissette)...225.00

10" Liesl (Cissette)..200.00

10" Louisa (Cissette) 265.00

Set of 7 dolls...1,400.00 up

Sound of Music, dressed in sailor suits & tagged, date unknown

17" Maria (Elise or Polly) 475.00

14" Louisa (Mary Ann) 475.00

10" Friedrich (Smarty) 350.00

14" Brigitta (Mary Ann) 375.00

14" Liesl (Mary Ann) 375.00

10" Gretl (Smarty) 350.00

10" Marta (Smarty) 350.00

Set of 7 dolls ....2,600.00 up

Sound of Music All in same oufit: red skirt, white attached blouse,

black vest that ties in front with gold thread ....each 350.00–500.00

Sound of Music, reintroduced 1992

8" Gretl and Kurt (boy in sailor suit)..each 62.00

8" Brigetta 55.00

10" Maria (Cissette) 85.00

12" Maria Bride (Nancy Drew) 132.00

South American 7" compo., 1938–1943 (Tiny Betty)...285.00

9" compo., 1939–1941 (Little Betty) 300.00

Southern Belle or Girl 8" hp., 1954 (Wendy Ann)..1,200.00 up

8" hp., 1955 (Wendy Ann)...750.00

8" hp., 1956 (Wendy Ann)...900.00

8" hp., 1963 only (Wendy Ann) 450.00

12" hp., 1963 only (Lissy)..1,200.00

#2155, 21" hp./vinyl arms., 1965, blue gown with wide pleated hem (Jacqueline)....................900.00

#2170, 1967, white gown with green ribbon trim 650.00

10" hp., 1968, white gown with green ribbon thru 3 rows of lace (Cissette) 425.00

1969, white gown with 4 rows of lace, pink sash 425.00

1970, white gown with red ribbon sash 425.00

1971–1973, white gown with green ribbon sash...425.00

10", My Doll House (see Special Events/Exclusives)

SOUTHERN GIRL 11–14" compo., 1940–1943 (Wendy Ann)..475.00

17–21" compo., 1940–1943 (Wendy Ann)..650.00–750.00

SOUTHERN SYMPOSIUM see M.A.D.C. under Special Events/Exclusives

SPANISH 7–8" compo., 1935–1939 (Tiny Betty) 265.00

9" compo., 1936–1940 (Litte Betty)..285.00

SPANISH BOY 8" hp., BK & BKW, 1964–1968 (Wendy Ann) 350.00

SPANISH GIRL 8" hp., BKW, 1962–1965, three-tiered skirt (Wendy Ann) 175.00

8" hp., BK, 1965–1972, three-tiered skirt...135.00

8" straight leg, 1973–1975, three-tiered skirt, marked "ALEX."..85.00

8" straight leg, 1976–1982, three-tiered skirt, marked "Alexander" 65.00

8" straight leg, 1983–1985, two-tiered skirt (1985 white face) 55.00

8" straight leg, 1986 to date, white with red polka dots (1986–1987 white face) 60.00

8" straight leg, 1990–1992, all red tiered skirt 55.00

SPANISH MATADOR 8", 1992 (Wendy Ann) 55.00

SPECIAL EVENTS/EXCLUSIVES Shops and organizations are listed alphabetically.

BELKS DEPARTMENT STORES

MISS SCARLETT 14", 1988 ....100.00

RACHEL/RACHAEL 8", 1988, in lavender gown...each 75.00

NANCY JEAN 8", 1990, in yellow/brown...75.00

FANNIE ELIZABETH 8", 1991, floral with pinafore...75.00

ANNABELLE AT CHRISTMAS 8", 1992, plaid, holds Christmas cards.....................................78.00

14" MISS SCARLETT
Made for Belk's Department Store, 1988

CELIA'S DOLLS
DAVID, THE LITTLE RABBI 8", 1991–1992 ....85.00

CHILD AT HEART
SCARLETT WITH TRUNK AND WARDROBE 8", 1989 (trunk and wardrobe added) 250.00
EASTER BUNNY 8", 1990, limit: 3,000 (1,500 blondes, 750 brunettes, 750 redheads) 365.00
MY LITTLE SWEETHEART 8", limit: 4,500 (1,000 blondes, 1,000 brunettes w/blue eyes,
    1,000 brunettes w/green eyes, 1,000 redheads w/green eyes, 500 blacks) 80.00

CHRISTMAS SHOPPE
BOY & GIRL IN ALPINE 8", in alpine outfits, limit to 2,000 sets 135.00

COLLECTOR UNITED
YUGOSLAVIA 8", 1987, F.A.D., limit: 625 ....125.00
TIPPI BALLERINA 8", 1988, limit: 800 ....400.00
MISS LEAH 8", 1989, limit: 1,000 ....225.00
BRIDE 8", 1989, F.A.D., limit: 500 (Betsy Brooks) 100.00
SHEA ELF 8", 1990, limit: 1000 ....200.00
WITCH/HALLOWEEN 8", 1990, F.A.D., limit: 500 (Little Jumping Joan) 145.00
NASHVILLE SKATER #1, (WINTER WONDERLAND) 8", 1991, limit: 350, F.A.D. (Black Forest) 185.00
NASHVILLE SKATER #2, 8", 1992, F.A.D. 85.00
CAMEO LADY 10", 1991, doll shop doll exclusive, limit: 3,000, white/black trim 125.00
RINGMASTER 8", 1991, limit: 1,000, F.A.D. (Lion Tamer) 200.00
CAMELOT 8", 1991, F.A.D. (Maid Marion) (Columbia, SC) 125.00
FAITH 8", 1992, limit: 900 ....325.00

DISNEY, WALT
CINDERELLA Annual Showcase of Dolls #1, 10", 1989, in blue satin, limit: 250 ....685.00
SNOW WHITE Annual Showcase of Dolls #2, 12", 1990, limit: 750 (Nancy Drew) 225.00
ALICE IN WONDERLAND/WHITE RABBIT Annual Showcase of Dolls #3, 10", 1991 ....325.00
QUEEN OF HEARTS Annual Showcase of Dolls #4, 1992, 10", limit: 750 ....400.00
BOBBY SOXER 8", 1990–1991 ....100.00
SLEEPING BEAUTY 12", 1990–1991 (Nancy Drew) 250.00
MOUSEKETEER 8", 1991 ....100.00

DOLL FINDERS
FANTASY 8", 1990, limit: 350 ....200.00

DOLLS 'N BEARLAND
PANDORA 8", 1991, limit: 3,600 (950 brunette, 950 redheads, 1,700 blondes) 85.00

DOLLY DEARS
SUSANNA CLOGGER 8", 1992, limit: 400 ....350.00

ENCHANTED DOLL HOUSE
RICK-RACK ON PINAFORE 8", 1980 ....300.00
EYELET PINAFORE 8", 1981 ....325.00
25TH ANNIVERSARY 10", 1988, long gown 175.00
BLUE BALLERINA 8", 1985, in trunk with extra clothes 185.00
VERMONT MAIDEN 8", 1990–1992, official Vermont bicentennial doll, limit: 3,600
    (800 blondes, 2,800 brunettes) 150.00
FARMER'S DAUGHTER 8", 1991, limit: 4,000 (1,000 blondes, 1,500 redheads, 1,500 brunettes)..150.00
FARMER'S DAUGHTER 8", 1992, "Goes To Market" (Cape and basket added) 90.00

FAO SCHWARZ
SAMANTHA 10", 1989 ....110.00
DAVID AND DIANE 8", 1989, in red, white, and demin, with wooden wagon ....set 150.00
BROOKE 14", 1989 (Mary Ann) 100.00
ME & MY SCASSI 21", 1990, all in red (Cissy) 350.00
SAILOR 8", 1991 ....80.00
CARNVALE DOLL 14", 1992 (Samatha) 190.00
BEDDY-BYE BROOKE 14", 1991–1992 ....165.00
SISTER BRENDA 8", 1992, sold as set only with BEDDY-BYE BROOKS ....set 230.00

First Modern Doll Club
    Autumn in N.Y. 10", 1991, limit: 260, F.A.D. (Gibson Girl)
      red skirt, fur trim cape, hat, muff skates 225.00

I. Magnin
    Cheerleader 8", 1990, F.A.D. 65.00
    Miss Magnin 10", 1991, limit: 2,500 (Cissette) 160.00
    Little Miss Magnin 8", 1992, with tea set and teddy bear, limit: 3,600 ....80.00

Imaginarium Shop
    Little Huggums 12", 1991, special outfits, bald or wigged 50.00–55.00

Madame Alexander Doll Club (M.A.D.C.)
    Fairy outfit 1983, for 8" non-Alexander 400.00
    Ballerina 8", 1984, F.A.D. 250.00
    Happy Birthday 8", 1985, F.A.D. 365.00
    Scarlett 8", 1986, limit: 700, red instead of green ribbon, F.A.D. 350.00
    Cowboy 8", 1987 ....500.00
    Flapper 10", 1988, black outfit instead of blue, F.A.D. 200.00
    Briar Rose 8", 1989, uses Cissette head 325.00
    Riverboat Queen (Lena) 8", 1990 ....375.00
    Queen Charlotte 10", 1991, blue/gold outfit, limit: under 900 ....375.00
    Prom Queen (Also called **Memories**) 8", 1992, limit: 1,100 ....375.00

Happy Birthday
Made for Madame Alexander Doll Club, 1985

M.A.D.C. Dolls, Exclusives (available to club members only)
   Wendy   8", 1989, in pink and blue 200.00
   Polly Pigtails   8", 1990 (Maggie Mixup) 175.00
   Miss Liberty   10", 1991–1992, red/white/blue gown (Cissette) 125.00
M.A.D.C. Symposium/Premier
   Scarlett   8", 1990, F.A.D. (white medallion – Snowflake Symposium;
      red medallion – Premier Southern Symposium)..285.00
      (Medallions: Midwest – rose; Southwest – peach; Southeast – blue; Northeast – lavender;
      West Coast – yellow; Northwest – green.)
   Springtime   8", 1991, floral dress, scalloped pinafore, straw hat, limit: 1,600 ....300.00
   Wintertime   8", 1992, all white, fur trim and hat (six locations), limit: 1,600 ....300.00
Madame Alexander Doll Company
   Melody & Friends   25", limit: 1,000, designed and made by Hildegard Gunzel,
      first anniversary dolls ....850.00 up
   Courtney & Friends   25" & 8" boy and girl, by Gunzel, second anniversary ....set 850.00
Marshall Fields
   Avril, Jane   10", 1989 ....195.00
   Madame Butterfly   10", 1990 ....90.00
Metroplex Doll Club
   Spring Break   8", 1992, 2 pc. halter and wrap skirt outfit, limit: 400 ....400.00
My Doll House
   Southern Belle   10", 1989, F.A.D. 125.00
   Queen Elizabeth I   10", 1990...145.00
   Empress Elizabeth of Austria   10", 1991, white/gold trim (Cissette) 145.00
New England Collector Society
   Noel   12", 1989–1991, porcelain Christmas doll, limit: 5,000 ....250.00
   Joy   12", 1991, porcelain Christmas doll 250.00
Neiman-Marcus
   Doll with four outfits in trunk   8", 1990 ....200.00
Sears-Roebuck
   Little Women   1990, set of six 12" dolls (Nancy Drew) ....set 375.00
Shirley's Doll House
   Angel Face   8", 1990 (Maggie Mixup) 125.00
   Winter Sports   8", 1991, F.A.D. (Tommy Snooks) 75.00
Spiegel's
   Beth   10", 1990, 1860's women...200.00
   Christmas Tree Topper   (Also called Merry Angel) 8", 1991 ....185.00
U.F.D.C. – United Federation Of Doll Clubs
   Sailor Boy   8", limit: 250 ....700.00
   Miss Unity   10", 1991 ....500.00
   Little Emperor   8", 1992, limit: 400 ....400.00
   Turn Of The Century Bathing Beauty   10", 1992, UFDC Region Nine Conference
      old fashion bathing suit, beach bag, and umbrella 300.00
Special Girl   23–24" cloth/compo., 1942–1946 ....450.00
Spiegel's   (see Special Events/Exclusives)
Springtime   8", M.A.D.C. (see Special Events/Exclusives)
Spring Break   Metroplex Doll Club (see Special Events/Exclusives)
Stilts   8", clown on stilts, 1992 ....60.00
Story Princess   15–18" hp., 1954–1956 (Margaret, Cissy, Binnie).....................................675.00
   8" hp., 1956 only (Wendy Ann) 1,500.00
Stuffy (Boy)   Hp., 1952–1953 (Margaret) 850.00
Suellen   14–17" compo., 1937–1938 (Wendy Ann) 1,000.00
   12", 1990 only, yellow multi-tiered skirt, Scarlett Series (Nancy Drew) 75.00

SUGAR DARLIN' 14–18" cloth/vinyl, 1964 only 100.00
   24", 1964 only 150.00
   Lively, 14", 18", 24", 1964 only, knob makes head & limbs move 125.00–165.00
SUGAR PLUM FAIRY 10", 1992, Portrette Series 92.00
SUGAR TEARS 12" vinyl baby, 1964 only. (Honey Bea) 95.00
SULKY SUE 8", 1988–1990, marked "Alexander" (Wendy Ann) 90.00
SUNBEAM 11", 16", 19" newborn infant, 1951 only 65.00–85.00
SUNBONNET SUE 9" compo., 1937–1940 (Little Betty) 300.00
SUNFLOWER CLOWN 40" all cloth, 1951 only, flower eyes 800.00
SUPERIOR QUINTS 8" compo. (made in Canada) ....each 100.00 set 550.00
SUSANNA CLOGGERS 8", Dolly Dears (see Special Events/Exclusives)
SUSIE Q Cloth, 1940–1942 ....650.00
SUZY 12" plastic/vinyl, 1970 only (Janie) 350.00
SWEDEN (SWISS) 8 hp., BKW, 1961–1965 (Wendy Ann) 175.00
   8" hp., BK, 1965–1972 ....135.00
   8" straight leg, 1973–1975, marked "Alex." 60.00
   8" straight leg, 1976–1989, marked "Alexander" 55.00
   8", 1986, white face 55.00
   8", reintroduced 1991 only 55.00
   BKW with Maggie Mixup face 250.00

8" SWEDISH
Straight leg, 1991

SWEDISH 7" compo., 1936–1940 (Tiny Betty) 265.00
   9" compo., 1937–1941 (Little Betty) 285.00
SWEET BABY 18½"–20" cloth/latex, 1948 only 40.00–50.00
SWEET BABY 14" "Sweet Tears," 1983–1984 ....55.00
   14" "Sweet Tears," reissued 1987, 1987–1991 (1991 has no bottle) 75.00
   14" in carrycase, 1990–1992 (1991 has bottle) 95.00–125.00
SWEET SIXTEEN 14", 1991–1992, Classic Series (Louisa) 120.00

SWEET TEARS 9" vinyl, 1965–1974 ....50.00
   With layette in box, discontinued 1973 ....150.00
   14" in trunk/trousseau, 1967–1974 ....200.00 up
   14" in window box, 1965–1974 ....145.00 up
   14" with layette, 1979 ....135.00
   14", 1965–1982 ....55.00
   16", 1965–1971 ....85.00
SWEET VIOLET 18" hp., 1951–1954 (Cissy) 700.00
SWEETIE BABY 22", 1962 only 145.00
SWEETIE WALKER 23", 1962 only 245.00
SWISS 7" compo., 1936 (Tiny Betty) 265.00
   9" compo., 1935–1938 (Little Betty) 285.00
   10" hp., 1962–1963 (Cissette) 1,200.00
SWITZERLAND 8" hp., BKW, 1961–1965 ....175.00
   8" hp., BK, 1965–1972 ....135.00
   8" hp., straight leg, 1973–1975, marked "Alex." 60.00
   8" hp., straight leg, 1976–1989, marked "Alexander" 55.00
   8", 1986, white face 55.00
   8" BKW (Maggie Mixup face) 275.00
SYLVESTER THE JESTER 14", 1992 (Mary Ann) 105.00
SYMPOSIUM M.A.D.C. (see Special Events/Exclusives)

8" SWEDISH, both tagged and have bend knees

Please read "About Pricing" for additional information.

TAFT, HELEN 1988, 5th set Presidents' Ladies/First Ladies Series (Louisa) 85.00
TEENY TWINKLE Cloth, flirty eyes, 1946 only 500.00
TENNIS 8" hp., BKW (Wendy Ann) 350.00
TEXAS 8", 1991 only, Americana 60.00
THAILAND 8" hp., BK, 1966–1972 (Wendy Ann) 150.00
    8" straight leg, 1973–1975, marked "Alex." 60.00
    8" straight leg, 1976–1989, marked "Alexander" (1985–1987 white face) 55.00
THOMAS, MARLO 17" plastic/vinyl, 1967 only (Polly) 600.00
THREE LITTLE PIGS & WOLF Compo., 1938–1939 ....each 650.00
THUMBELINA & HEE LADY 8" & 21", 1992, limit: 2,500 sets 550.00
TIERNEY, GENE 14–17" compo., 1945 (Wendy Ann) 1,400.00
TIGER LILY 8", 1992 (Wendy Ann) 55.00
TIMMY TODDLER 23" plastic/vinyl, 1960–1961 ....150.00
    30", 1960 only 200.00
TINKERBELLE 11" hp., 1969 only (Cissette) 600.00
    8" hp., 1991–1992, Storyland Series, has magic wand 65.00

14" BETTY TAYLOR
First set of Presidents' Ladies/First Ladies Series

Tiny Betty 7" compo., 1935–1942 ....285.00
Tiny Tim 7" compo., 1934–1937 (Tiny Betty) 300.00
    14" compo., 1938–1940 (Wendy Ann) 575.00
    Cloth, early 1930's 650.00
Tippi 8", 1988, C.U. (see Special Events/Exclusives)
Tippy Toe 16" cloth, 1940's 600.00
Tom Sawyer 8" hp., 1989–1990, Storybook Series (Maggie Mixup) 90.00
Tommy 12" hp., 1962 only (Lissy)...1,200.00
    15" hp., 1950–1952 (Little Men) (Margaret, Maggie) 800.00
Tommy Bangs Hp., 1952 only (Maggie) ....800.00 up
Tommy Snooks 8", 1988–1991 only, Storybook Series (Wendy Ann)..55.00
Tommy Tittlemouse 8", 1988–1991 only, Storybook Series (Maggie)..55.00
Tony Sarg Marionettes Compo, 1934–1940 ....245.00 up
Topsy-Turvy Compo. with Tiny Betty heads, 1935 only 165.00
    With Dionne Quint head, 1936 only 300.00
Toulouse-Lautrec #2250, 21", 1986–1987 only, black & pink 195.00
Trapeze Artist 10", 1990–1991, Portrette Series (Cissette) 95.00
Tree Topper 8", 1992, red/gold 80.00
    8", 1992, multi-laced skirt 70.00
Treena Ballerina 15" hp., 1952 only (Margaret) 750.00
    18–21", 1952 only 900.00
Truman, Bess 14", 1989–1990, 6th set First Ladies/Presidents' Ladies Series (Mary Ann)..............100.00
Tunisia 8", 1989 only, marked "Alexander" (Wendy Ann) 80.00
Turkey 8" hp., BK, 1968–1972 (Wendy Ann) 135.00
    8" straight leg, 1973–1975, marked "Alex."..60.00
    8" straight leg, 1976–1986, marked "Alexander" (1985–1986 white face)............................55.00
Tweedledum & Tweedledee 14" cloth, 1930–1931 ....each 700.00
20's Traveler 10", 1991–1992, Portrette Series, M.A. signature logo on box (Cissette)..............74.00
    25th anniversary, 1982, Enchanted Doll House (see Special Events/Exclusives)
Tyler, Julia 1979–1981, 2nd set Presidents' Ladies/First Ladies Series (Martha) 105.00
Tyrolean Boy & Girl* 8" hp., BKW, 1962–1965 (Wendy Ann) ....each 200.00
    8" hp., BK, 1965–1972 ....each 135.00
    8" straight leg, 1973, marked "ALEX." ....each 60.00
    8" BKW, (Maggie Mixup) ....each 225.00

Became Austria in 1974.

Please read "About Pricing" for additional information.

U.F.D.C. Sailor Boy 1990 (see Special Events/Exclusives)

United States 8" hp., 1974–1975, straight leg, marked "Alex." 50.00

    1976–1987, straight leg, marked "Alexander" (1985–1987 white face) 55.00

    1988–1992 (Maggie face) 50.00

Union Officer 12", 1990–1991, Scarlett Series (Nancy Drew) 80.00

    8", 1991 only, Scarlett Series 85.00

Van Buren, Angelica 1979–1981, 2nd set Presidents' Ladies/First Ladies Series (Louisa) 105.00

Vermont Maid Enchanted Doll House (see Special Events/Exclusives)

Victoria 21" compo., 1939, 1941 (Wendy Ann) 2,200.00

    21" compo., 1945–1946 (Flavia) 2,300.00

    20" hp., 1954 only, Me & My Shadow Series (Cissy) 1,400.00

    14" hp., 1950–1951 (Margaret)...1,000.00

    18" hp., 1954 only, slate blue gown, Me & My Shadow Series (Margaret) 1,300.00

    8" hp., 1954 only, matches 18" doll (Wendy Ann)..1,200.00

    14" baby, 1975–1988, 1990–1991 ....95.00

    18" baby, 1966 only 100.00

    18" reintroduced, 1991 ....85.00

    20" baby, 1967–1989 ....50.00–60.00

    20" in dress/jacket/bonnet. 1986 only 95.00

Victorian 18" hp., 1953 only, blue taffeta and black velvet gown,

    Glamour Girl Series (Margaret) 1,400.00

Victorian Bride 10", 1992, Portrette Series 105.00

Vietnam 8" hp., 1968–1969 (Wendy Ann) 350.00

    1968–1969 (Maggie Mixup) 375.00

    8", reintroduced in 1990–1991, (Maggie) 55.00

Violet (see "Sweet Violet").

Violetta 10", 1987–1988 (Cissette) 75.00

Please read "About Pricing" for additional information.

W.A.A.C. (ARMY) 14" compo., 1943–1944 (Wendy Ann) 750.00
W.A.A.F. (AIR FORCE) 14" compo., 1943–1944 (Wendy Ann)..750.00
W.A.V.E. (NAVY) 14" compo., 1943–1944 (Wendy Ann) 750.00
WALTZING 8" hp., 1955 only (Wendy Ann) 600.00
WASHINGTON, MARTHA 1976–1978, 1st set Presidents' Ladies/First Ladies Series (Martha) 275.00
WELCOME HOME–DESERT STORM 8", mid-year introduction, 1991 only,
    boy or girl soldier, black or white 75.00
WENDY "LOVES BEING LOVED" 8" doll and wardrobe, mid-year introduction, 1992 only 105.00
WENDY (FROM PETER PAN) 15" hp., 1953 only (Margaret) 650.00
    14" plastic/vinyl, 1969 only (Mary Ann) 300.00
    8", 1991–1992, Storyland Series, slippers with pom-poms, no faces 55.00
WENDY ANGEL 8" hp., 1954 (Wendy Ann) 1,200.00
WENDY ANN 11–15" compo., 1935–1948 ....500.00
    9" compo., painted eyes, 1936–1940 ....325.00
    14", in riding habit, 1938–1939...400.00
    14" swivel waist, any year 450.00

14" W.A.A.C., 1940's   **17" WENDY ANN, 1930's**

17–21" compo., 1938–1944 ....650.00–850.00
14½–17" hp., 1948–1949 ....850.00
16–22" hp., 1948–1950 ....850.00
20" hp., 1956 (Cissy)..525.00
23–25" hp., 1949 ....825.00
8", 1989, first M.A.D.C. doll (see Special Events/Exclusives)
WENDY BRIDE 14–22" compo., 1944–1945 (Wendy Ann) 275.00–325.00
15–18" hp., 1951 (Margaret) 350.00–400.00
20" hp., 1956 (Cissy)..450.00
23" hp., 1951 (Margaret) 600.00
8" hp., 1955 (Wendy Ann)...350.00
WITCH 8", 1992, Americana Series 55.00
WITCH/HALLOWEEN C.U. (see Special Events/Exclusives)
WHITE RABBIT Cloth/felt, 1940's 500.00–600.00
WILSON, EDITH 1988, 5th set Presidents' Ladies/First Ladies Series (Mary Ann)...............85.00
WILSON, ELLEN 1988, 5th set Presidents' Ladies/First Ladies Series (Louisa) 85.00
WINNIE WALKER 15" hp., 1953 only (Cissy) 245.00
18–23" 375.00
In trunk/trousseau, 1953–1954 ....800.00 up
WINTER SPORTS 1991, Shirley's Doll House (see Special Events/Exclusives)
WINTER WONDERLAND 1991, for C.U. (see Special Events/Exclusives)

13" JANE WITHERS, 1937
(Autographed on tummy)

WINTERTIME M.A.D.C. (see Special Events/Exclusives)

WITCH 8", 1992, Americana Series 55.00

WITHERS, JANE 12–13½" compo., closed mouth, 1937 ....950.00

    15–17", 1937–1939 ....1,200.00

    17" cloth body, 1939 ....1,300.00

    18–19", 1937–1939 ....1,300.00

    19–20", closed mouth 1,400.00

    20–21", 1937 ....1,800.00

1860's WOMEN 10" hp., 1990, Spiegel (see Special Events/Exclusives)

YOLANDA 12", 1965 only (Brenda Starr) 325.00

YUGOSLAVIA 8" hp., BK, 1968–1972 (Wendy Ann) 135.00

    8" straight leg, 1973–1975, marked "Alex." 60.00

    8" straight leg, 1976–1986, marked "Alexander" (1985–1986 white face) 55.00

    8", 1987, Collector United (see Special Events/Exclusives)

ZORINA BALLERINA 17" compo., 1937–1938 (Wendy Ann) 1,500.00

Schroeder's
ANTIQUES Price Guide

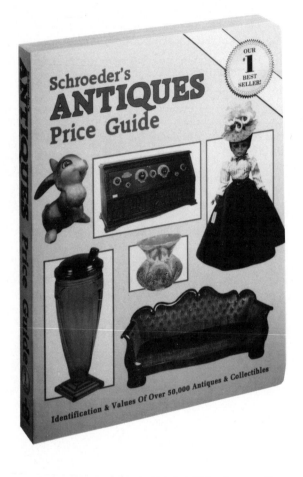

Schroeder's Antiques Price Guide is the #1 best-selling antiques & collectibles value guide on the market today, and here's why . . . More than 300 authors, well-known dealers, and top-notch collectors work together with our editors to bring you accurate information regarding pricing and identification. More than 45,000 items in almost 500 categories are listed along with hundreds of sharp original photos that illustrate not only the rare and unusual, but the common, popular collectibles as well. Each large close-up shot shows important details clearly. Every subject is represented with histories and background information, a feature not found in any of our competitors' publications. Our editors keep abreast of newly-developing trends, often adding several new categories a year as the need arises. If it merits the interest of today's collector, you'll find it in *Schroeder's*. And you can feel confident that the information we publish is up to date and accurate. Our advisors thoroughly check each category to spot inconsistencies, listings that may not be entirely reflective of market dealings, and lines too vague to be of merit. Only the best of the lot remains for publication. Without doubt, you'll find *Schroeder's Antiques Price Guide* the only one to buy for reliable information and values.

8½ x 11", 608 Pages   **$12.95**

COLLECTOR BOOKS
A Division of Schroeder Publishing Co., Inc.